TILL DEATH DO US PART

A CIVIL WAR STORY

By

Gary L. Steel

ISBN: 0-7596-9521-0 (softcover)
ISBN: 0-7596-9520-2 (ebook)

This book is printed on acid free paper.

Edited by Jean Champagne, Manchester, NH

1stBooks - rev. 03/08/02

INTRODUCTION

A BIOGRAPHICAL JOURNAL

This is a story about one man's experiences while serving in the Union Army from 1862 to 1864. It is what happened to a Pennsylvania man from Blair County—Altoona, Pennsylvania. That man was Samuel G. Steel, who volunteered for service in the late summer of 1862 for a nine-month term. He would serve with the 125th Regiment, Pennsylvania Volunteer Infantry.

This term with the Army of the Potomac he would live through what was called the Maryland Campaign and one of the bloodiest battles of the war, Antietam. He would move with the army doing what was asked of him and finish his enlistment in the spring of 1863, after the Battle of the Wilderness in Virginia.

At the end of the Gettysburg Campaign he found himself volunteering again, this time for a three-year term. He would be a paid substitute for another man, drafted into service with the 149th Regiment, Pennsylvania Volunteer Infantry. This was a special unit of the Army of the Potomac called the Bucktails. They were sharpshooters and scouts as well as combat infantry veterans.

He would suffer all the hardships of this war like every other man—the bad weather, sickness, fatigue, hunger, and the heartache of being separated from home and family. This term he would head south with the army in pursuit of Robert E. Lee and the Army of Northern Virginia.

He would make many new friends and lose many more; while he'd watch generals come to lead the army, only to be replaced for their failures by another. When Ulysses S. Grant took control, he realized there would be no turning back from the enemy now. The terror of war was all around him again. The only thing to do was obey orders and to try to survive this great conflict between the North and the South.

This story has been written based on documented facts and figures, taken from military records, books and articles on the Civil War, family records and writings of the time, and other sources including the History of the 125th and the 149th Pennsylvania Volunteer Infantry Units.

Many of the occurrences described in this story were everyday life to the common soldier. This is a reflection of one who was there at those times and places.

WRITER

GARY LYNN STEEL

GREAT, GREAT GRANDSON OF SAMUEL G. STEEL

Samuel's second wife, Martha, sometime around 1875

CHAPTER 1

HOME and FAMILY

The year was 1890. It was a very hot August day with temperatures in the ninety-degree range. A brief summer shower had just passed through and cooled the air slightly as Sam sat on his front porch watching. He could see for miles up and down the valley through the haze of the hot afternoon. But now the steam from that shower, evaporating from hot sun-baked earth, was rising and filling the valley with a low hanging mist.

Sam had just come in from the barn and garden before the shower came, where he was overseeing and trying to be of as much help as he could to his wife Martha and some of their children. The weeds in the garden were thick this year due to the manure that he and the boys had spread that spring, but the vegetables were doing just fine. They were all looking forward to eating more of their harvest as it matured and to the endless canning, preserving, and storing of it for the long cold winter.

Martha was a very hard worker, and the chores never seemed to end; but she never complained. She was a loving mother and a good wife to Sam. Differences in their ages didn't seem to matter at all. She was fourteen years younger than he, and she was his second wife. Martha

Isabel was born in 1846 and married Samuel G. Steel in 1873. They had five children. Starting with the oldest, there were Oliver Logan, Charles Walter, Hugh Lynn, and, lastly, twins Emma Rebecca and Ida Marion.

Sam often thought about his first wife. It was hard not to because he could see her image in all of his older children. Catherine and he had been married in 1855 in Blair County, Altoona, Pennsylvania. His and her families were from the area, and she was two years his senior. Catherine came from the Champino family, which happened to be direct descendants of the Cherokee Indian nation. They were very much in love and suffered through one of the worst periods in the nation's history. In the time that they were wed, Catherine bore him six children starting in 1856 with George Edward. Then there were John Jordon, Harry Anderson, Matilda Ann, Mary Elizabeth, and finally Samuel Franklin, born in 1870. In April of 1873 Catherine passed away, leaving Sam with a house full of motherless children. He knew something had to be done like getting married again.

The late afternoon was getting even hotter as Martha ran here and there trying to make sure that everything was just right for tomorrow's dinner. She had contacted their children not at home and invited them to a family gathering, and all were coming. With the grandchildren, she would be feeding eighteen hungry mouths.

Sam's two oldest daughters, Mary and Matilda, would be arriving any time now. They were coming together before their husbands arriving the next day in order to help

Martha with all the preparations. Sam was sitting on the porch watching down the road when he saw a carriage coming in his direction. He could not see who it was at that distance, but he told Martha that he thought her help was finally on its way. After a few minutes the carriage was close enough that Sam could see his two daughter's smiling faces, and he went out to greet them. After squeezing and hugging him until he turned pink, they ran to the house to see Martha, leaving Sam to tend to the horse and carriage. After that was done he returned to his rocker on the porch.

Out of Sam's eleven children, two would be absent but not forgotten. They were Harry Anderson, who died of fever in 1865, at the age of four and a half and John Jordon, who passed on in 1879 in his mid 21st year—both children with Sam's first wife.

As Martha and the girls worked, they knew it would be a long, hot, busy evening with baking piecrusts and fresh bread. She knew they needed a little more help, so Sam was called from the rocking chair on the porch to choose a prime cured ham from the root cellar and to make sure Charlie was working the butter churn properly and not daydreaming, The evening passed quickly, and it was after midnight until they could retire. They still had a lot of food preparation to do in the morning.

Sam woke early, with all the noise and chatter coming from the kitchen, no one, unless he was deaf, could sleep. He woke slowly to the smell of coffee drifting in from the kitchen where Martha was preparing breakfast; and he did not want to miss any of it, as he was as hungry as a bear.

He stuck his head around the doorway, still in his nightshirt, and asked "How soon?" Martha replied, "Lots of time yet. You go ahead and get cleaned up for the day."

Sam relaxed. His washbasin was all ready and even his shaving brush and straight razor were laid out for him. He finished up, got dressed, and into the kitchen he went. It was a fine breakfast of pancakes, eggs, bacon, and coffee. Martha told him she wanted to feed him well because it had to keep him until the noonday meal, which would be a little late because of everyone's arrival. After he was done eating and finished a second cup of coffee, she gave him some last-minute instructions and scooted him out the door, telling him on his way out to keep busy this morning and stay out of the kitchen. There was too much to do, and she didn't want him underfoot. He felt like a scolded dog, but as he turned to gaze back through the screen door, he could see the twinkle in Martha's eye and the grin on her lips.

There he stood on the porch thinking of what Martha needed. He was to get a couple of small buckets and go get the pie fillings for the dessert. She wanted berries and apples picked, enough for three pies. Sam knew just where to go. So he headed out with his containers down the dusty road leading from their house. It would take a while to get enough berries for a pie, but he would get them first. The apples would be easy. As he came to the first bushes along the road, he could see a lot of the ripe fruit hanging in bunches, and he started picking away. There were some not ripe yet, and their bright color was pretty.

As Sam moved down the road picking, he jumped two large rabbits from the weeds and watched them hop away, thinking if he only had his shotgun they would be easy targets. As he continued picking, a noise caught his attention. He looked down the road and saw Mr. Wright approaching in a wagon pulled by an old worn-out looking mule. As he got to Sam, he stopped the beast and gave him a "Good Morning!" greeting. Sam needed a break anyway, so he thought they would talk a while. Mr. Wright owned the property around Sam's farmhouse. Sam asked if it would be all right to pick some of the apples in the field above the barn. Mr. Wright smiled and replied, "Sure, if they aren't picked they will just be left for the deer." Sam had bought his property from Mr. Wright and thought now was the perfect time to inquire about purchasing more. He told Mr. Wright that a couple of his older boys would like to take up a little farming with him to make some extra money raising corn and maybe a few beef cattle. He asked if he was willing to sell and the answer was yes. "Good" Sam said. "The boys will be around today, and we will talk it over and get back to you." With a firm handshake they parted, and Sam went back to picking. There, that looked like enough to him.

Now for the apples. He headed back toward the barn and into the field beyond, to a fencerow crossing the hill where the apple tree stood. As he waded through the tall weeds, he could imagine rows of corn standing there. As he came to the trees, he was startled by the sudden appearance and snort of a large buck jumping up in front of him. It ran slowly away jumping the fencerow and heading into the woods, looking back at him briefly. Sam thought he saw at least eight points and thought again of hunting. He gathered the bucket of apples, some from the ground and others knocked from the tree with a long stick, and headed back. When he got to the house he set the pails down on the porch, and Martha was there in a flash. She looked into the pails and said, "That should do nicely—thank you, Sam," and went back into the kitchen.

He knew what was going to be needed now. He had to make sure there was enough seating and table space for all the food and people and perhaps a little extra in case a friend or two of the family dropped by. Right now he was going to sit on the front step, relax a little, and think this through. After a while it came to him, a good plan. With a little help he could add to the picnic table in the back yard under the shade trees. There were sawhorses and planking in the barn and some larger firewood-length tree-trunk pieces for benches.

At this point he was quite proud of himself and thought that wasn't so bad and leaned back to rest a bit. A few minutes later Charlie and Hugh came out onto the porch after eating their breakfast, and Sam set them to work gathering up the needed materials. Sam knew this would take the boys a while, so he stood up, stretched to relieve some old aches and pains a little, and slowly made his way to the backyard where the work was to be done. The boys were working like crazy, bringing all that was needed. Sam supervised the project to be sure it was sturdy enough for the day. In no time it was completed to their satisfaction, and the boys were off to the nearby creek for some entertainment until the families arrived.

It was well past mid-morning now, and the family should be gathering soon. The sun was getting high in the sky, and the heat of day was building. Sam looked around. All was quiet in the shade of the spreading oaks, so he thought he would step over to one of his old tool sheds to see what he could find. When he got there he opened the door and was greeted by a very angry swarm of wasps. One managed to land on his nose, and before he could even blink an eye, the deed was done. At this point, Sam was furious and with a hoe handle he knocked the nest down and smashed it, his nose stinging and thumping like a drum. He finished off the few remaining beasts. The only thing he could do was pack some cool wet mud on the wound and wait for the pain to subside.

Now with both eyes watering, he could see through the tears what he had come for—some of his private stock he had hidden from Martha. He thought to himself, if I ever needed a drink, it was now. It was rye whiskey. He removed the cork from the jug and took a long drink. It seemed to help the pain. He replaced the jug after putting an ointment of rye on his wound and a fresh layer of mud then slowly returned to the tables. He was glad no one was watching what just happened, but the evidence would be easy to see. He was afraid his nose would swell to the size of an elephant's and his eyes would swell up, so he would have the look of a mole. The only thing he could do was to keep something cool on it and relax. About an hour later, after many mud packs, Sam went to the water trough at the barn to wash the topsoil from his nose and look at his reflection. His eyes and nose still felt a bit puffy, but they did not look as bad as he thought. Either the rye or the mud had helped.

Now the family was arriving in wagons, buggies, and on horses. There was a flurry of hugs, and handshakes, and greetings all around. The women all flocked to the house to help with last-minute preparations, while the men waited for a few latecomers.

They sat in the shade of the picnic area, smoking and talking while Sam sucked on the fresh chew of tobacco he had just stuffed into his cheek. They talked about their jobs and friends at work, Sam not missing a word, wanting to know everything that was transpiring in his families' lives. He listened mostly, asking an occasional question to hold the interest in the subject at hand. After a while Sam brought up the situation involving the chance to buy more ground and asked if any of them were still interested in doing so. As he let the idea sink in, he turned his head and discharged a shot of tobacco juice six feet across the yard and turned back to the boys with a streak running down his chin. With a wipe of his hankie, he was soon back in order and waited for the answer. After some thought, the young men agreed it was a good investment; if their work held through the winter months, they could afford to do something about it in the spring. Sam sat back with a satisfied look on his face and agreed with them, saying he would talk to Mr. Wright first chance he got and see to the details. If things went well they could do some farming in the spring, even if it meant a small down payment to close the deal. Sam would take care of it so plans could be made.

During their talk Sam Jr. couldn't help but notice there was something unusual about his father's face, and he asked if he was doing okay with his health. Right away he knew what he was talking about and started to explain as they stood and walked over to the tool shed. As Sam finished the story about the wasp nest, he opened the door and grabbed the jug, saying to the other men, "We will just take a little nip, it will give you an appetite for the meal that is coming." The jug was passed around and then gently put back in its place with the anticipation of returning to it later in the day.

Everyone had arrived by now, and the picnic table was being covered with food, the women carrying out plates and bowls of all kinds filled to the top. As the men came closer they could smell the aroma of all the food and feel their mouths begin to water as their eyes fell upon it, especially the still warm baked pies sitting at the end of the table.

Once they were all together, they said the blessing for the meal and began the feast. The afternoon passed quickly with delicious food, lively talk, and lots of laughter. The children were playing games, and the men were all gathered around that little tool shed of Sam's. After cleaning up, the women sat and chatted, drinking lemonade and looking out across the yard to the shed where the men were laughing and telling stories.

As the men talked, they would take turns stepping to the side where the jug was kept to take a swallow and return to the group and the story telling. They consisted of

Sam senior, Sam Jr., George, the oldest boy, and two of the son-in-laws. As time passed the tales of hunting and fishing became more outrageous. One story got quite a laugh when Sam Sr. told it to the boys. It was about a deer hunt he was on a few years back with some of his friends. He was invited to a place that was sure to be full of big bucks to kill and everyone would get one for sure, so Sam was told. When he got to the spot where he was told to stand and watch, he got situated among the trees and waited, thinking this wouldn't take long.

According to the property owner, there would be plenty of chances to bag a big one. Sam liked to chew tobacco and often had a little residue on his chin. While he waited for a buck to pass by, he did some considerable chewing. He waited and spat and waited and spat and finally after a lot of chewing and spitting, he saw the only deer of the day in the late afternoon. The deer was just walking slowly through the trees; not knowing Sam was there taking aim at him. Sam said with emphasis, "Boy it was a big horned deer!" holding his arms outstretched wide. Sam continued, "When he got within thirty yards of me, be stopped broadside and looked in the opposite direction, letting me get a more comfortable position to shoot from. As I raised the gun to sight him, I stepped forward a little and squeezed the trigger." Everyone stood spellbound listening to the story end right there. Sam said no more and walked to the side of the shed for a swallow of rye. When he took his place again, everyone asked him what happened next. He looked down at the ground and said, "I shot under him by a mile. I had spit so much tobacco juice on the ground where I stepped, I slipped and the gun went off." With that, everyone laughed heartily and each had another round of rye.

The men had nothing over the women when it came to talking. Two of Sam's oldest daughters, Matilda and Mary, were telling all about the modern conveniences that could be found in the cities like Altoona nowadays. Things like gaslights and indoor plumbing in homes that could afford such things, even new stoves with hot water tanks to supply the bathtub.

They talked about everything available in the stores and shops from china-head dolls to jewelry and piece goods or fashions. The ladies weren't quite sure what the attraction was to that old shed until it was time to go home. When the men returned to the picnic area, it was obvious what they were doing. Sam's nose was red and his eyes were glassy. Sam Jr. and the rest of the men were not much better. They didn't have any problem with their wives driving the horses home that evening.

The next morning Sam woke earlier than usual, as he had a long nights rest due to staggering to his bed early the night before. He woke with a feeling of urgency, that something was wrong, not knowing exactly what had happened last night. He listened to the normal sounds coming from the kitchen and decided to venture out. Martha was at the table, ready with a cup of strong coffee. Sam sat down with a sheepish grin and most gladly took the cup. Martha looked up, smiled, and asked, "How do you feel this morning?" With that Sam relaxed a little and answered, "Just fine." He somehow knew that things were all right after all. Martha and the other women accepted the fact that on occasion the men would drink way too much. It was a fact they had come to deal with.

They began to talk quietly because everyone else was still sleeping. Martha remarked about what a good time everyone had the day before, and they would like to do it again—maybe in the fall, perhaps during hunting season. Sam looked up from his coffee and said he thought that was a good idea. As they chatted they could hear the rest of the household begin to stir. They heard the twins quietly making baby talk to each other as they awoke, talk that only Ida and Emma could understand.

They were just about a year and a half old now and full of energy. Sam looked at his wife as the thought crossed his mind, and he said, "You know, it is not unheard of, but a bit unusual, that yesterday some of my grandchildren here were older than some of my children." They were all half brothers and sisters; it was a mix of ages and origins from Sam's two marriages, but he was proud of them all and they got along well together.

Sam was not yet ready to eat this morning, thought he would get out of the house for some fresh air, and let Martha do her business at hand. He went out onto the porch and sat down. It was cooler than the day before; and the humidity had left, and the air was clean and clear. Now he could see the far-off mountains with great detail. It was peaceful here in the valley. He could see the little village of Calvin, which was located in Huntingdon County. They had lived here for just a little over five years now, and they really liked it. Sam had bought the property in 1885 from a local farmer. The purchase consisted of a one-and-a-half-story farm-house, a barn, several small sheds, and a little under an acre of ground. It needed some fixing up before they moved from Altoona, and that's where the older boys really pitched in and helped. With the cost of the property and repairs, it set him back. It took a month and a half of his army pension checks to pay for it all that amounted to just about $45.00. As Sam sat in his rocker, he thought it was well worth the money.

About that time the two youngest boys came out after eating their breakfast, and Sam stopped them to give some instructions for the morning chores. First, they were to put back the temporary table and seating that was used the day before, and then see to the milking and feeding of the animals before venturing off this morning. He would talk to them later.

After the boys left, Sam sat back again to rest. He was no longer a young man. This coming winter on December 25th, he would be fifty-eight years old. The previous years of hard work and dealing with life's troubles had taken their toll. Right now he was still a little tired from the recent activity and fun. He could feel the aches in his joints and muscles and especially in his left hip and leg. Sometimes he looked down and imagined he could still feel it, the leg that had been missing from the knee down for over twenty-five years. Now he was used to it, the peg leg that helped him get around with the occasional assistance of a crutch. He began to think back to the days in Altoona when he was working for the Pennsylvania Railroad in the blacksmith shops. As his mind wandered, the clarity of the present time and place started to become farther and farther away, until finally all thought was on past life experiences and what had shaped his life.

Samuel G. Steel just before the war

CHAPTER 2

THE WAR

Samuel had been working for the Pennsylvania Railroad for a number of years, even before his marriage to Catharine. It was late in the year of 1860, and the turmoil and problems of the nation were coming to a head. Rumors of war and the final separation of the country was all the talk and on everyone's mind. It was next to impossible to ignore it and everyone's opinion on the subject. With the coming of the new year, something was going to happen. No doubt about that.

In November of that year, after the election of Abraham Lincoln, is when troubles started to escalate rapidly. Sam read newspaper articles, from assassination threats on the president, to the beginning of secession of the southern states. Of the thirty million people in the United States at that time, about two-thirds lived in the north. The remaining one-third lived in the south, four million of them being slaves. On December 20th, South Carolina seceded from the union. After that, on January 9th, Mississippi—so on it went. Sam could not believe what he was reading sometimes in the papers, especially of the election of Jeff Davis as president of the Confederate States of America in February of 1861.

Winter passed for Sam and his small family without too many daily problems. It was a harsh, cold winter as usual in the Altoona area, with snow and ice piling up along the streets and sidewalks. Sam spent a lot of his spare time shoveling out himself and some of his neighbors. Even at the railroad shops, teams of men had to clear areas of the stockyards with shovels and sleds to remove snow for heavy traffic spots. Many men came down sick during this time because of the temperature changes from the shops to the outside when even on the coldest days the men would sweat working in the ironworks environment and walk home after a hard day at work in the cold and damp. Sam was no exception. He came down with a cold or the sniffles several times. At their house most of the rooms got chilly during the day, but the kitchen and dining room stayed warm from the cook stove that Catherine kept working all day long, either cooking or heating water for her laundry or cleaning purposes. There was always a large kettle with a spout for pouring, setting under the bread warmer on the back of the stove.

Sam's work did not end when he left the shops. When he got home he had to go to the back yard to split wood for the cook stove and carry it into the back porch off the kitchen along with buckets of water from the hand-pump well for daily house-hold use. In the evening after eating, the cook stove was left to go out, and a larger wood and coal stove would be fired up. It was located in the center of the house attached to a fireplace flue. Sam had to keep it supplied with wood and coal and keep it free of ashes. It made a lot of extra housecleaning for Catherine in the winter, but it was a much needed heat source.

Time went by for the family, and now it was the last week of March and the weather was becoming much more pleasant and signs of spring were in the air. The daylight hours were becoming longer; and when April came, Sam got the gardening bug, with spring fever. He was anxious to get started and spent a beautiful Saturday afternoon spading up their garden patch in the backyard, getting it ready for some early vegetables such as onions, radishes, and peas. Sam figured he would have plenty of room for the rest of the garden crops after these were picked and stored. His routine was pretty much the same day by day until the news of Fort Sumter hit the town.

The newspapers over the next few days were filled with the battle of Charleston Harbor and about the assault on the Federal units on the morning of April 12th. The Rebel bombardment resulted in Anderson's surrender. The celebrations throughout the South were everywhere over their victory, and Virginia, which was one of the largest and most populated states, was going to secede any time now. On the 15th of April, Sam saw the headlines in the paper reading that Lincoln declares war. Meanwhile, attacks on Union Garrisons in the South were growing.

Out of the hundreds of men that worked in the shops with Sam, many were talking about joining the army right now and ending this rebellion once and for all time; most of them thinking it would be no problem and would be over soon enough. A lot of the men volunteered right away and were given a leave from work to go, but Sam had thoughts about the situation. He wanted to stay with his family for now and see what would come out of this whole mess. He stayed working at the shops for the next year keeping up on the news of the war and much of it was first-hand knowledge. Some of the men who had gone off to Fort Sumter had been returning to work with their ninety-day term of enlistment up.

Sam was hearing the stories and reading all about them every day. The first great battle of Manassis (or Bull Run) he knew was a Union defeat and was saddened by the fact that 22,000 Rebels had beaten and forced to retreat—37,000 Union men led by General McDowell. Names like Jackson and Beauregard were associated with the victors, the Union loosing 5,000 men in the battle on July 21st, 1861. In August, a new Union army commander took over. It was General George B. McClellan, now with 100,000 men in the Army of the Potomac. Sam knew a lot of the new men were from Pennsylvania. Meanwhile, he read stories about the war in the west. Things seemed to be going a bit better for the Union forces there, on and around the rivers leading to the Mississippi and the South. The front was being extended to 1,000 miles in length around the Confederacy. By the end of 1861 there were over 700,000 men in the armies of the Union.

The news of war was quiet that winter except in the west with reports of scattered skirmishes and Union army occupation of many cities and towns. Now with spring coming, Sam saw stories of Grant's movements in Kentucky and Tennessee and the bloodbath known as Shiloh where 100,000 men fought on the banks of the Tennessee River. These stories were about navy battles in

March of the Ironclads, the Monator, and the Maramack and the movement of the Army of the Potomac, finally, after eight months of setting still. The papers said that President Lincoln was insisting McClellan advance on the enemy now and whip him. Sam read the news about the Virginia Peninsula movement with 110,000 men and the stalling of the army on May 20th close to Richmond. He heard in late June about the fighting that started around that area, and that by the end of the first week in July the Army of the Potomac was running scared, back away from Richmond.

That wasn't the only bad news. The papers were also reporting three Union armies in the Shannondoah Valley were being beaten and harassed at every point from Winchester south, by a man called Stonewall Jackson. Again 20,000 Rebels were thrashing 40,000 Union men. Sam was deeply worried about the fate of the Union army along with everyone else and that a new man who replaced Johnston, named Robert E. Lee, had beaten McClellan's and his army would be known as the Army of Northern Virginia from now on.

Winchester, Virginia, wasn't that far away. Sam kept thinking to himself that the enemy is strong enough in that area to fend off the Union Army. What if they were to bring their army farther north? The fighting would be too close for comfort. Stories of scouting and raiding much farther north were being reported, and this was a constant worry to everyone. Most of the men in the area knew that a local militia force would not stop any kind of invasion of a well-trained and led army. They were beginning to find out more about this man Robert Edward Lee than they wanted to know. It was common knowledge that many of the leaders and generals of the south were former Union soldiers and West Point graduates, Lee being one of the best. It was also the fact that the Lincoln administration wanted Lee to take command of the Union forces in the beginning when Virginia seceded. He turned down the job to go with his home state. After being a military advisor to Jeff Davis, he moved into an active field command position and was starting to show his talent as a leader. Most men knew that mil itary or not, if you had a determined, aggressive leader to follow it made all the difference in the world.

Many of Sam's co-workers had joined later after Bull Run, in order to wrap things up at home before leaving. One of the returning soldiers in March of 1862 was a man by the name of Jacob Szink. Jacob was a bubbly, enthusiastic young man that Sam knew from work. He had worked for the shops about five years before Sam started and was well known and liked. He returned from service with the rank of Captain and was very proud of that fact. Almost right away he started his recruiting efforts and talked all about the adventures that could be had. After several months of listening to this, Sam had a change of mind. He and Catherine had been talking about his enlistment for months. She was not in favor of it and wanted him home.

By this time the stories of the war were not looking very good for the Union, and this was constantly on Sam's mind. He wanted to do something to help. After long hours of talking to his wife, she finally gave in. If she didn't she would never hear the end of it. The next day Sam went to Jacob, who was still trying to recruit enough men for a company, and started to ask questions. Jacob was quite the talker and convinced Sam to sign up.

It was July 28th, 1862, and he had signed his name Samuel G. Steel to the register of Volunteers to the 125th Regiment, Pennsylvania Infantry. Jacob shook his hand and said it wouldn't be long now, the unit was just about formed and to settle matters at home as soon as possible for they may be leaving for Camp Curtain in Harrisburg, Pennsylvania, to be mustered into service within the next week to ten days.

Sam finished out the day at work and headed home. On the way he started to worry, wondering if he had made the right decision. He had signed up for a newly created nine-month enlistment outfit, and it was starting to make him think just how long and lonely nine months away from home would actually be and if he would ever come home at all.

That night he and Catherine talked a long time, crying on occasion from both of them. He would miss her terribly and the birth of their new baby. She was due about mid November. That week passed much too quickly for both of them. Sam was feeling a little better about leaving though, after all he was going with a lot of men he knew well, all from the Blair County area; and his job and family would be there when he returned. Catherine's family was close if she needed anything.

The next day after work, Sam informed his supervisor and took his leave from work. He and a few friends had agreed to help each other out when they could, trying to get things in order at their homes before leaving. They took wagons to the woods for several days cutting and hauling as much firewood as they could to supply their homes for that coming winter. Coal was another essential item on the list. Some men had sons or family at home old enough to take care of such things, but in Sam's case, he didn't; and in Catherine's pregnancy he did not want her overdoing things. He wanted to make it as easy as possible for her. He made some needed repairs around the house and spent a couple of evenings making sure the garden was spotless of weeds.

The day before Sam was scheduled to leave, the families got together to see him off and wish him well. It was just a short visit, and cake and coffee were given to the guests while they talked. As they sat around the table discussing matters, Sam was reassured that everything would be in good hands during his absence. As Sam looked around the table at both families, there was quite a contrast. His folks were blue-eyed, light skinned persons while Catherine's were dark eyed, dark skinned people with high cheek bones and raven black hair. They were all good people, and Sam felt comfortable being around them. After they said good-by and left, Catherine and Sam spent a quiet evening at home together with their children; and Sam got a few things together he would need to take with him when he left in the morning.

The train pulled out of Altoona on the morning of August 8th, heading for Harrisburg. It was very crowded with other units from the surrounding counties. They arrived at Camp Curtain and waited there for their equipment and supplies. Sam was beginning to understand the old saying that he had heard from some of the veterans, of the army being a "hurry up and wait" organization. Now he saw it.

The camp consisted of a few permanent, large buildings and tents as far as you could see. The men spent about five days just lying around, going to eat several times a day, and standing in line most of the time waiting for one article of equipment to be given out. By the end of that week they were fully equipped and ready for the next phase of their journey.

On the 15th of August 1862, Sam would muster into service with all his friends, officially, as the 125th Regiment, Company D, Pennsylvania Infantry Volunteers. Captain Jacob Szink was put in charge right away and promoted to Major of the Regiment, so he made the choices for the rest of his officers he would need in his chain of command.

The next day a train was boarded again, packed with soldiers heading through Baltimore, Maryland, to the defenses around Washington. First stop was Camp Wells, where Sam and the rest of the Regiment would be getting their first few weeks of training. Time went pretty well for the men. They weren't soldiers yet, but with the endless drills, discipline training, more drills, discipline, learning bugle calls, and all that goes with orders in the army, they were learning to be soldiers. During this time Sam had made a lot of friends from the surrounding counties, and they were getting ready to move again. This time they were moving to a fort called Banard, also in the Washington defenses area. There the food was a. little better, and things were much cleaner and a bit slower moving. Maybe now Sam would have time to write a few letters home and let Catherine and everyone know where he was at the time and what he was doing.

It was now September 6, 1862, and the Regiment had become a part of the Army of the Potomac, First Brigade, First Division XII Corps. By the sound of that the men felt like they now belonged to something more important and permanent, and they even had a mailing address. Sam finally got a letter written to Catherine, satisfied now that she would be hearing from him and that he was doing well. In his letter he described everything that had happened since he left Altoona and how much each day he was missing and loving them. He also told Catherine to write, and he should get the letters sometime in route wherever he was moving to.

He went out to put it with the rest of the outgoing mail. On his walk-through the fort, he could not help noticing a great commotion at the headquarters with officers coming and going. When he got back to his company, the word was out that Lee's army had crossed the Potomac River a couple of days ago in strong force, and the Regiment was going to be on the march. What was Lee doing? Where was he going? What and where were they going was the question on everyone's mind. The Regiment got together their equipment, three days' cooked rations for each man, rifles, and backpacks. They went on the march that afternoon. The only thing Sam knew was they were headed out in a Northwest direction and were going to link up with the rest of the division somewhere. As they marched along the first few miles, all the men were not saying a word to each other, just listening to officers shouting to close ranks and keep it moving. After about five or six miles they were ordered to the side of the road to rest and let the wagons catch up. They had started out later that afternoon needing to load up.

During this break they had time to grab a bite to eat from their rations and talk awhile, speculating on what lay ahead of them and where they were going. Sam sat down in a field along side some of his buddies and dug out some hard tack to munch on. He knew how rough it was to eat without assistance from some kind of moisture, other than sucking on it until it softened or just testing the strength of your teeth and jaws. The thing a lot of men did was to soak it in water before trying to eat it. They were nothing but flour, water, and a little salt mixed and baked to the texture of a brick.

As the break went on, some groups were playing cards, some were sleeping, and others were talking about the strategy of battles, the way they saw it. As Sam listened to some of the talk, he had to laugh to himself, thinking there sure were a lot of imaginary generals in this outfit. Sam saw that the crowd was thinning a little around the small creek that was nearby, and he thought he would go and fill his canteen while he had the chance. While he was there, he took time to rinse some of the sweat from his face and neck. He was surprised to find the water so cold this time of year and thought he would take a walk up stream and look around, to be by himself for a few minutes. He walked along the little stream for a distance when he saw why it was cold. There were three openings in the earth where underground springs were coming to the top, flowing crystal clear. There he stood for a while just looking around and admiring the beauty of nature and the peace and quiet.

Before heading back, he took a long, cold drink from the spring and headed out feeling refreshed and a bit cleaner than before. As he made his way back to the road, he could hear the sounds of the army and went back to his spot in the field. It didn't take long for the wagons to catch up; and they were moving again, this time behind the wagons. They would go ahead to a predestination to be ready for camp that night. Following the wagons wasn't much fun. They ground the road into a dust; and every foot of the way the road powder floated in the air, covering the men. By sunset they were camped within shouting distance of the Potomac River. They had moved parallel to it all day and did not know it. Sam had friends in the outfit; but he marched near a boy named John McCarthy about all day, and they were quickly becoming friends. He found that John was from Huntingdon County, Pennsylvania, and they shared a few common interests.

They set up camp that evening, and John decided to stay with Sam. After setting their tents and collecting wood for the campfire, they were ready to get their evening meal.

They went to their company's mess areas to receive rations for the night and the next morning's meals. Each company had its own supply wagons, so Sam and John separated to collect what they needed. As the men moved through the line they were told that this might be the last hot meal they would have for a while, and they would be pulling out early. Sam filled his haversack with hardtack, dried beans, coffee, salt, rice, and bacon and was given a chunk of meat that was just butchered that day and partially boiled.

John met him back at the tents, and they began cooking. After the fire was hot enough, Sam secured his meat on the end of a stick and roasted it over the flames while they soaked their beans in water for tomorrow. After eating they decided it would be a good idea to cook their bacon while they had hot coals. That evening they sat around the campfire and talked while listening to all the sounds from the camp activity—men talking, laughing, along with the rattle of pots and pans, and an occasional "whinny" or "moo" from the livestock. As Sam was moving towards his tent to retire for the night, he scanned the scene and saw thousands of campfires dotting the countryside as far as he could see. Lying down inside his tent, he quickly fell asleep.

The bugles sounding off woke the army early. Sam and John stoked up their fire for coffee and a quick breakfast. They boiled beans in their coffee pot when it was empty and ate a quick meal before taking down the camp. Sam said he would clean up the cookware while John returned the tents to the wagons. Sam went to the riverbank to fill their canteens and clean things up. When he got there, he wasn't alone. There were thousands lining the banks doing the same thing. The only cleaning method available was to rub the utensils with riverbed sand to cut the bacon grease and food particles. It was crude; but after rinsing, they came out quite clean and shiny.

They were on the move early in a fog-shrouded landscape, but it wasn't long before the hot sun burned it away. As they walked, Sam and John passed the time talking. Now they were linking up with other Regiments and Brigades, but the officers kept things moving right along. Stories of South Mountain and other places Sam had never heard of before started to spread down the line along with battles that were going on. No one knew the whole truth; they were just moving where George McClellan was telling the generals to go. Sam thought they had gone about five miles and was glad to be stopping for the night.

After making their usual preparations for the night, Sam and John walked around, stopping at intervals to listen to the talk of the day at every gathering of men. Now that so many units were in the same area, the stories were wide-ranging and numerous. One of the things they heard repeatedly was that Lee had an army with him much larger than the Union and that McClellan was calling for more men. This was hard for Sam to imagine, with the ocean of men he was with, that a larger ocean could be waiting to face them. The thought of it was bewildering and scary. He looked at the faces in the firelight gathered round, each group they stopped at showing every emotion known to exist, from fright to joy. Each group, without fail, had its loudmouth saying he was not afraid of anything or anyone and to bring on the fight. Neither Sam nor John said a word. They both knew that when the fight started, attitudes like that were likely to change in a hurry.

The hour was getting late so they headed back to their tents and got ready to sleep for a few hours. Morning would be here before they knew it and another day of marching. They were on the move again early the next morning. After ten miles they stopped and camped again. This time they were waiting for further orders to come. Divisions were together this time; everywhere you looked. For miles "There was army," as John put it. They were starting to become more familiar with generals names and their reputations, both North and South and were well aware of several, especially the enemy. Names like Lee, Jackson, Longstreet, Hill, and Stuart were names that put fear in a bunch of green privates like Sam and John.

After setting up camp and resting a bit, the bugle call was heard summoning the men for company formations. They gathered in the fields close to the road and were assembled with the rest of the Regiment of the 125th. Each company had its own officers posted in front, and the men were told there would be an inspection of equipment and ranks first thing in the morning. Also, the word was to be ready to move at any time. The officers said it could be tomorrow or in a couple of days; it would depend on the orders expected from high command. They were dismissed, and they returned to their campsites. Men sat around camp that evening polishing, brushing dirt and dust from coats and trousers, and cleaning weapons. They were checking cartridge boxes, canteens, haversacks and all, to make sure everything was in good order and supplied.

Early in the morning, the sound of bugles brought the men out of their tents before sunrise. They stoked up their fires and ate the first meal of the day. It wasn't long until they were called into formation for inspection and the orders for the day. Inspection went well; and some of the deficiencies were corrected then—such things as rations and cartridges—while there was time to do so. Before they were dismissed, assignments for duty were given to each company in the regiment. Squads of about ten men each were assigned guard duty for the duration of the encampment, working in three different shifts. Sam was put on guard post duty, starting that night at midnight until 8:00 a.m. As luck would have it, John's company drew the same task, and the two of them would be working together.

While they waited at camp for their time to come up, Sam and many of the men took time to write letters home to their loved ones. As Sam wrote to Catherine, he was concerned about the threat to his life in battle, but he didn't want to express it, knowing she was worried enough. Instead, the letter was on the lighter side of things, telling her about the friends he had made and the country he was seeing.

The time came to go to headquarters for the changing of the guards. It was a clear, cool night, and the rising full moon was lighting up the countryside, casting long shadows and making it easy to get around without the need for lanterns. Company D and H were posted along the road near the river on the south side of camp. At about 3:00 a.m., when the harvest moon was just overhead, the light from it was overwhelming. It was so bright that anything moving or still could be seen without a problem. Sam would stand awhile in one spot and look at the countryside bathed in moonlight, then walk up and down the road for a distance in each direction. On one trip he met John standing at the end of his post. They talked quietly a little while, and then went back to the job. The stillness of the morning was unbelievable, knowing the tens of thousands of soldiers were right there within a short distance.

It was about 4:30 a.m. when Sam could see the approach of a man coming his way on the road, and it brought every one of his senses to a peak. He knew what his job was, and when the unknown figure was close enough, Sam stepped out and challenged the man, asking, "Who goes there?" The answer came back, "Sergeant of the guard." Sam told him to come forward and be identified. Sam could clearly see the man's face and knew he had done his job. He reported that all was quiet there and with that the sergeant moved on.

The moon was fading away with the coming of dawn; and the air was cold and still, leaving everything wet with dew as the sun rose. It wouldn't be long now until Sam would be relieved, and he would go back to camp. That time came and John joined Sam for breakfast and a cup of coffee. After reporting to headquarters, they found out they were on the same duty again, at the same time, only in a new area. This time they were to watch the river. They walked back to their tents in the warm morning sun, drying out from the dew soaked night and went to sleep quickly.

They were both up and around before dark that evening and sat talking with others who came by. When the time came to go, they went to headquarters for duty and were sent out with lanterns because clouds had moved in and were blocking out the moonlight. They went south of camp again, but farther this time to the river, where Sam took his post. The morning hours went by uneventfully, with occasional breaks in the clouds letting moonlight cast beams to the darkened landscape and putting a shimmering glow to the water in front of Sam.

When morning came, Sam was relieved and went to camp for upcoming duty orders. After finding out that they were being replaced by other companies for guard duty, they were told to stand down and wait for word to come. With that they returned to the tents to rest, eat, and see what would come next.

After a couple of days, word came to move because Lee was moving near a town called Sharpsburg, Maryland. Now the Army Corps was on the move. The mood of the men was changing slowly as they went; smiling faces had turned to serious looks of thought and concern. Something was going to happen and soon. This was September 15th, and they were coming closer to this place called Sharpsburg. Then they came to a halt and were told to rest and eat. Their company's officers would be along to tell them the situation and what to expect.

CHAPTER 3

ANTIETAM

The day had melted to early evening, and the men gathered in Company groups, some sleeping, others eating, and still others writing letters home, which was just what Sam and John were doing when the officers were seen riding down the road towards them. John jumped up and said, "I'll see you around, Sam, I have to get back to Company H with the rest of the fellows," and off he flew. Sam just nodded his head in reply and gathered with Company D, as nervous as the rest of his buddies.

He recognized the face right away. The officer, still on the horse in front of them, was Jacob Szink, who he hadn't seen since leaving Altoona. He was a Lt. Col. now to the men and still had a twinkle in his eye and a smile for his friends. He addressed them in a loud clear voice saying, "Men," he hesitated a moment, looked around at all the eyes of anticipation and slowly started. "Men, there is going to be a battle, a very big battle, possibly tomorrow." He paused; there wasn't a sound in the crowd. "The Army of the Potomac is here. We are about 87,000 strong. We, the XII Corps, are second in line of battle. The Army of Northern Virginia is just over those hills. From our reports we think they number from sixty- to ninety-thousand; we cannot be quite sure. This may be a hard couple of days, men. Your Company commanders will be telling you more in the morning. Now eat, get some rest, and God bless you all." Then he was gone. There was stillness for a minute; all the men looked at each other, saying nothing. Then someone yelled, "Let 's kick some Rebel ass, tomorrow!" With that, everyone cheered and the mood lightened.

Camp was set, and campfires lit the sky in every direction. Sam and some of his comrades sat around their fire talking and joking as they checked their equipment they would need for tomorrow and tried to imagine what it would be like. Sam just thought—I guess I will know more tomorrow. The morning of September 16th came, and the first meal of the day was over and more rations passed out. The word was that the I Corps was getting ready to move out. It would take time to move so much equipment and men so that the XII Corps would have no problem getting ready to follow.

During their wait to move out, John came over to where Sam was sitting along the side of the road and began to tell him about his life back home where he grew up on a farm.

He was twenty-three, just five years younger than Sam and seemed to be drawn to him for some reason. Whether it was for advice or just the big brother influence, Sam wasn't sure, but he liked him and didn't mind at all.

John talked about missing his family and having eight brothers and sisters. He said he was next to the oldest of them and had a lot of responsibility keeping up the farm. Sam was quite impressed when he was told John was a schoolteacher, also. He worked the farm in the summer and taught in the winter. Their farm was near the little town of Airy Dale, located in Huntingdon County, Pennsylvania, just about eight miles east of the county seat. He told Sam he would have joined up sooner, but his Dad was in poor health and needed him at home. They were a poor family, but all the children went to school and were smart. John was not married, but he had a sweetheart; and they were going to get married as soon as this was all over. Sam talked about his life in Altoona with his wife Catherine and their small children and some about his work at the railroad shops there. Their talking ended with the appearance of their officers calling out orders to form up. They parted to join their companies in the movement.

On they went, clouds of dust filling the air along with all the noise that comes from a moving army. It was late in the day when they were in the position ordered. They were behind and to the left of 1st Corps, ready as they ever could be, they thought. From where Sam was he could see only trees and Union soldiers in front and a clearing or two in the distance beyond. He had never been in war before. He was weak in the knees, and he felt little tremors vibrate through his body, uncontrollable nerve tension. He took a deep breath and looked around. He found out he wasn't the only one. One man to his right was down on all fours, throwing up. Then it started. First it was musket fire in the distance, getting more intense at times, and then slowing down. Now cannons began to ring out. This was just a little after 6:00 p.m. if Sam's pocket watch was right. This went on back and forth the rest of the daylight hours. It had to be the I Corps.

Just about 9:00 p.m., it started to drizzle rain, soaking both armies, but sporadic firing went on all night. Sam did not sleep at all that night. Everyone was told to sleep on his arms, and he just tried to keep warm and dry. The sound of the battle seemed to calm him a bit, strangely enough, so now he could sit and rest.

The dawn was coming; there was no stopping it. Sam was up pacing back and forth amongst the trees and had a path worn smooth in the dirt from his nervous strides. It was very foggy now as the sky began to lighten, and it started again. This time it became twenty times worse than before—cannons, muskets, but still not close. He felt safe for now. He could see smoke rolling up all over the area in front both right and left. This kept up for two hours without a let up, and about 8:00 a.m. his division was ordered to start forward. He would be in the lead elements of the XII Corps. It took almost an hour to get to a point where he could begin seeing flashes and smoke directly in front at a distance. The advance was getting hit with cannon from long range and some small arms fire. Now he saw something else. Men in gray uniforms at a distance moving away, turning and firing, and moving again. He did not know where he was, but it was thereafter known as the East Woods.

The first brigade was ordered out of the woods. They could see a cornfield to the right or what was left of one, and now Sam began to see what the results of all the noise was. Now there was a dramatic slowdown in the firing. Sam gazed with all the others as they passed a forty-acre field of cut-down corn and men as well. The sight was unreal to look at—so many bodies. Some still moving piled over the top of each other, blue and gray alike for as far through the field as could be seen. At a glance it could have been thousands. No one took time to stare or count; they were under fire now themselves. The Brigade was getting separated in the confusion. The 125th was ordered to lie down in the field. Sam didn't waste any time. As he lay there thoughts of what he had just seen did not seem of this earth; it was not real.

Puffs of dirt began to leap up in front of him, the strange zing of lead close to his ears. It was rifle fire from the Rebs. An officer came up on horseback ordering them to their feet, to fix bayonets, then he shouted, "Forward," and again, Forward!" They could see a small white building about 600 yards across the open field and that was their objective.

They moved at a steady, fast pace towards the white building that was just inside a heavy tree line. Resistance was light, just sporadic musket fire. When they made it to the trees there was no enemy resistance. Different companies were assigned to check things out. One went to the white building and reported that this church was full of Confederate dead and wounded. Another went deeper into the woods and set up defensive positions. The rest stayed on guard at the tree line. Sam was at the tree line. Now they all moved into the trees; the time was just after 9:00 a.m. The men of the 125th did not know the danger they were in. They had advanced on their own to a position right in the middle of the enemy lines, and the wounded in the church were part of Jackson's Corps. There they stood alone. Just about now one of Sedgwick's Division was leaving the East Woods and crossing the open field toward the West Woods, right where the 125th was located; but this movement by part of the II Corps did not go unseen. Their lead element was the 34th New York. That regiment came in behind and to the left of the 125th. The remainder went into the woods behind the 34th. Sam, John, and the rest of the 125th didn't feel so alone at this point.

The XII Corps consisted of about 10,000 men in its infantry units, but Sam knew they were scattered all around the area and that some were being held in reserve back behind the lines. Right now they were all wishing they had those men right there. On their way to the West Woods they passed so many dead soldiers of both sides. It was hard to know where they were from. They only knew it was the I Corps men, and the gray uniformed men were from all over the South, such as Texas, Arkansas, North and South Carolina, and Georgia. Some of the bodies were no longer recognizable as human forms. They were simply blown apart by canister shot or the exploding artillery rounds, or their bodies just fell apart when hit by volleys of musket fire. Sam couldn't get the sight of all this to leave his mind while he waited in the woods. Will this happen to me? he thought. Will I wind up being one of those mangled bodies among thousands of dead, not even being known who I once was? With these thoughts a sudden change took place within him. It was a rising feeling of hate mixed with fearlessness and of defiance. He couldn't stop it, and he didn't want this feeling of courage to end. He knew this is what it takes to be in a battle and defend your life. It was a basic animal instinct to survive.

As Sam looked at the men around him, he could see that he was sharing this moment with all of them. As he turned back to his own thoughts again he double-checked his equipment and took a drink form his canteen; and as he replaced it, the loud shout of the sergeant behind him rang out, “Here they come!”

Now all hell broke loose. A massive unseen Rebel attack hit like a sudden wave. To Sam it seemed like a bolt of lightning when hundreds of muskets went off all at once right at him and around him. Cannon fire—no time to think, just point and fire. They were everywhere, running, screaming, ducking, hiding, and coming back up. They loaded and fired repeatedly. Officers were yelling commands that now could not be heard. There was no time to even think, if you wanted to survive. You had to fight. You could not take an eye off the enemy for a second, except to reload and hope the man firing in your turn was doing some good. Killing wasn’t as hard as he dreamed it would be, not now, not here, with slaughter going on everywhere around him. It was insane. Blood spraying all around, chunks of bone, brains and all happening so quick. Sam stood and fired into a mass of gray coming right at his line. When the gun went off he had killed two with one shot. He crouched down to reload, and the men behind stood and fired. Now the front line stood and fired off a volley. Seconds later about half of them were riddled with holes; the bowel contents of the man to the front left of Sam flew in his face. Now they were everywhere again, endless streams on the left, in front, on the right, moving past, firing on the New Yorkers in behind. You could shoot only one direction at a time. Men were hit at all angles. What remained of the 125th were lying flat to reload and firing from the ground. The roar was deafening; nothing mattered but surviving.

Their faces were turning black from burnt powder, and heat waves were rolling off the rifle barrels from repeated firing. Sam watched one of his own men in line trading off rifles with some of the fallen men in order to get a cooler barrel to work with. So he started doing the same thing; and two of them he picked up were all ready to fire, with their owners being dead or too badly wounded to fight any longer. Sam found himself back-to-back with three other men. It was an automatic move governed by the situation of being surrounded. They were protecting each other from the screaming Rebel yells in all direction. They continued swapping rifles and firing at the gray masses.

Men were running low on ammunition and grabbing cartridges from dead men. Some were rushed so badly, they didn't take time to remove the ramrod; and it went to the target with the ball. They were still caught by three sides, the enemy line to their front stopped in place, giving the 125th time to load and regroup their thoughts. The Rebs had to stop; from all the smoke, they could not see more than twenty-five feet ahead of them. They knew the Yankees were there but not how many. Through the smoke came a shout, "Throw down your arms and surrender!" Sam thought, "NO! Go to hell, not on your life!" About then a man in front of Sam stood, shouting back, "Come and get us!" All three ranks fired in order, and a moan went up less than fifty yards away. A lieutenant stood up in the back line, shot through the shoulder, and yelled for the 125th to retreat to the left and rear. So they left, down on ammunition and strength. The lieutenant saw a break in the assault, and it was now or never. On the retreat from the woods, bodies were scattered around everywhere. One in Sam's path caught his attention. He looked quickly and then had to move on at the run. It was John, his new friend, staring straight into the sky with a hole in the center of his forehead. They ran across the open field back towards the East Woods, hoping not to catch one in the back.

As they ran, some men were being hit from artillery rounds and bullets. It was a confused, running mass of men from different Corps and Divisions. One bunch of men running about fifty feet in front of Sam just flew into pieces when they were caught in a blast of canister shot from a Rebel battery. They ran as fast as their exhausted bodies could take them. When they were within their own lines, they collapsed to the ground. They were out of action the rest of the day. When Sam recovered himself, he found two holes in his clothing—one in his hat and one in his sleeve, but no injuries. The battle would rage on all day long, the sounds moving from right to the far left.

Sam was hearing all kinds of stories now coming back with the retreating units of men. He was learning about all the loss of life and how the first Corps had been wrecked so badly and that the XII and II hadn't faired much better. It was only estimates of the numbers, and the battle was still raging. The 125th Regiment was trying to find its surviving members and regroup itself back behind the lines of men who were being held in reserve. It took over an hour for the remaining officers to get the companies back in the area; and when this was done there were entire ranks missing, some with only one man standing in them. Everyone was hoping that more would show up soon, but only a few stragglers came in; and they were wounded, putting them out of action. As Sam looked around, it seemed like about forty or fifty percent were missing. The official count was not yet known. They were dismissed from formation and told to be ready if needed, but everyone knew it would not happen. Plenty of troops were in reserve to handle about anything that could happen.

Sam and what remained of Company D went back to a clearing near a field and rested while they ate and tried to clean themselves up. He had lost a lot of friends this day, and the reality was starting to settle in as he lay stretched out on his back and looking up at the sky and listening to the battle roar on and on. His day was over now, and Sam felt a strange calm within. He had seen hell itself and lived to see tomorrow. That fight at the church lasted less than thirty minutes, but it seemed like forever. As he lay there on the ground, his mind was beginning to remember sights and sounds in more detail. There were so many things happening in such a short time that his senses had stored them somewhere in his brain, and now they were coming back like flashes of light. He remembered seeing several strange acts by men while in the peak of battle at the church. There were men who froze in place, not able to move, or even defend themselves. They just stood or crouched down with a blank look on their face until they were shot or run over by moving troops. One man stuck in Sam's mind, especially. He was in the heat of the fight along with everyone, when Sam glanced over and saw him standing facing the enemy with his head bent down like he was in prayer at church. With lead flying all around in sheets and trying to fight back the enemy in their advance, Sam had only a couple of opportunities to glance over in the direction of this strange sight. During the course of several minutes, each time he saw the man, he was in the same position. After loading and firing again and again, which took some time to accomplish while trying to stay protected yourself, the man was still there untouched by what was going on around him. A few minutes later, when looking in that direction, the man was nowhere in sight. He was either captured or finally came back to his senses and took cover to fight or pray from.

Sam knew that many of the scenes he had witnessed that day would come back to haunt his thoughts and dreams forever. With the stress and activities of the last couple of days and the lack of rest and proper food, many were falling asleep now even with all the noise of the battle. Sam was no exception. He rolled onto his side and drifted off to sleep. A few hours later the steady rumble woke him up and back to the presence of danger. He looked around and saw many men still sleeping. He got to his feet and stretched out the kinks in his body, listening to the sounds of fighting still going on in the distance. It was becoming late in the day now, and he managed to stop a few Privates who were walking by to ask what was happening. The men told him of what they had heard, and they thought it to be true. They told him about the sunken farm road that the

Rebels were defending and how the Union had suffered so many losses taking that position and so many Rebels had suffered; they were calling it "Bloody Lane" now. The other story was about Burnside's men trying to take the high ground on the other side of the lower stone bridge across the Antietam Creek. They knew he suffered many losses getting over, but he finally made it. But now with all the sounds coming from that direction, it didn't seem like a very good place to be at. After telling Sam what they knew or thought to be fact, they moved on.

As the remainder of the daylight hours passed, the sounds of the fighting began to subside slowly. By evening it was down to a few scattered shots here and there. Sam rested by the campfire with the men in his company as they all thought of what tomorrow would bring. As they looked out into the darkness of the distant hills, they could see many campfires lighting the sky with their orange glow and knew the enemy was still in fact waiting for them. "Well," Sam said to one of the men, "There is no sense worrying about it any more tonight. We should get our rest and be ready for it tomorrow, whatever it is." With that, everyone settled down with their rifles by their sides and went to sleep on the ground around the fire.

Monument dedicated to the 125th Pennsylvania Regiment Volunteer Infantry, located at the Antietam Battlefield, Sharpsburg, Maryland

CHAPTER 4

AFTER THE BATTLE

The morning of the 18th dawned bright and clear. Sam's outfit was being held in reserve now. The battlefields were almost silent but for an occasional shot or two. Pickets were posted, and the remaining officers were trying to get numbers together and reorganize broken units. Sam and some of his few remaining buddies were together having coffee and rations when word came that Lee's army had pulled out during the night back across the Potomac, but they still had a strong rear guard in place. Sam sat and began to think. The 125th had lost so many of their members yesterday. He lost too many friends, and he was determined not to be so involved with other men's lives anymore. That way it wouldn't hurt so much when they were gone.

As the morning passed, Sam was watching the wagons and teams of men gathering the dead and wounded from the blood-soaked battlefields when a sergeant from one of the other companies came by and asked for volunteers with the stomach to help with the clean up. No one said a word at first. Sam thought, why not, I'll help because when my time comes I know I will welcome it if need be. So he stepped forward toward the sergeant and said, "I will, Sir." With that, two more men came forward, and they left for detail. They found out many of the living had been gathered during the night with the aid of lanterns to see. Now their orders were to search for the living and tend to the dead last. Sam and his group were told to look for any living among the hundreds of bodies in their assigned area of the field. As they were checking each one, Sam saw every kind of mutilation that could be imagined, from missing heads to half bodies. As they moved through the field, the wagons behind them were filled to capacity and replaced with empty ones stained with blood from their gruesome cargo. Sam found many dead men that looked like they had just fallen asleep on the ground; with no sign of injury except when he touched them, he knew the rigid stiffness meant no hope. After checking about fifty bodies, both blue and gray, the smell was starting to make Sam a little queasy in the stomach, and he took a walk away from it for a few minutes to get some air.

As he stood watching, something was quite puzzling to him. Many of the dead had no shoes, and some had shirts and trousers missing. The sergeant of the detail walked over to Sam, stood by him, and asked how he was doing. Sam said, "Okay, just needed some time." The sergeant said, "Don't think you're alone with that thought. We all feel the same." As they stood and talked, Sam found out that the Rebel soldiers had robbed the dead of any valuable items they could find. Sam was sure that this practice wasn't just all Rebel soldiers either, but they were the major offenders because of their lack of supplies. Everything was taken, from money to diaries and bibles.

This made the identification of many of the dead impossible to determine.

Sam went back to work with the rest, and the second body he checked was different. When he pulled on the man's arm to roll him over, it pulled back in reaction to his touch. He knelt down beside the man and turned him over to find a nasty head wound. The man was still alive, but he could not talk or move. Sam shouted to the stretcher-bearers, and they came and took the man away in the direction of the field hospital. After about four hours of this duty, they were being replaced with men from the other reserve units, and they returned to the rear to join their company. By this time it was getting late in the afternoon, so they settled down for the evening for some much needed rest.

As the evening passed, Sam sat by the fireside with the others and leaned his tired back against a tree. He listened to the conversations going on all around him for a long time. The subjects varied greatly. He started to doze off, and the voices began to fade into a jumble of low-toned sounds getting farther and farther away. When he finally woke up the camp was quiet. Everyone was sleeping, and the fire was about out. He got to his feet, stretched a little, and looked at his watch in the dim light of the fire, finding it to be 12:20 a.m. Now he was fully awake and put more wood on the fire to take the chill away. Finding himself alone now, he began to feel the deep sadness and heartbreak of being away from home and all that he loved and missed. The stress and tensions of the recent events were taking their toll on him now. He sat by the fire and cried and cried until his weariness finally put him to sleep.

The 19th they were on the march, heading for the Harpers Ferry area, so they were told. It was a long day's march, and they were hearing results now of the battle. From the evening of the 16th to the evening of the 17th, they had lost well over 12,000 men and estimates were about the same for the enemy. As they were moving out of the battlefields of Antietam, they could still see many bodies lying in the open fields in rows. These were the dead of both sides not yet gathered up. The wounded were still being moved to field hospitals where they were being treated. The air had the smell of rotting flesh everywhere, and as they passed several of the hospitals, the scene was the same. Each had a pile of dead men lined in a row outside, and on the opposite side was a pile of decaying legs and arms, removed by surgeons in great haste. Many men bowed their heads; some looked away as they marched. It was unbelievable to everyone. They settled down in camp that night at Maryland Heights and waited.

The men had plenty of time for writing and receiving letters from home. The fall weather was fine, and the colors of autumn were beautiful. They waited and waited. During this time the army was reorganizing. The first brigade was now the second. Sam wrote home about it and received his first letter from Catherine. He was glad to hear everyone was fine, and his wife was getting along well with her pregnancy.

It was now the first week of November. The weather was getting colder, and camp life was boring. Lots of men were sick, and a few had deserted. Many in the Regiment were building winter quarters. Groups of men were getting together and building what amounted to a small log cabin with chimneys for fires. The tents they were staying in would be quite uncomfortable when snows came. Sam and three other men got to talk about their shelters for the winter and decided to work on one together. They made a plan to put all four of their one-man tents tightly together, back-to-back, and enclose them on three sides with a shelter or a windbreak of sorts. They knew by now from many of the veterans, the army was always unpredictable about its moves and that helped in making their decision not to go to all the work with a log shelter.

They started by planting four poles in the ground the size they wanted the shelter. Then they used the ax they had to cut smaller trees for roof rafters and sidewalls, tying them together with rope. Then on top of that they wove in grapevines gathered from the woods. They did this on the three sides facing the winds from the West. Now they added the final finishing layer of pine boughs to thatch the roof and walls. When it was finished they had room at the opening to set up a fire pit for cooking and some heat.

Now it was finished, and they were pleased with it. Sam said it wasn't very pretty, but it would shed most of the snow and ice of winter and block the winds just fine. They were leaving camp, but they would be back. They were moving to the Shenandoah Valley on a reconnaissance mission just to look around and let their presence be known and then return in a couple of weeks. It was a welcome break in the boredom.

Their first day of marching took them in a southwest direction. A small cavalry squad and artillery units with field guns accompanied the infantry. Along with that came the wagon train with supplies to last a few weeks. It was an uneventful couple of days heading towards the town of Winchester, Virginia. They didn't seem to be in any sort of rush to get to any place special, so the pace was easy to keep up. From what they were told, there would not be any major engagements fought if they could be avoided and to expect some resistance if the enemy made an appearance. They knew the Confederate Army was in the area around Winchester and that the town had changed hands several times with occupying armies. They were swinging to the Southeast of town and heading toward the mountain ranges due south.

About the fourth day out, part of the cavalry squad reported seeing Rebel horsemen at long range and their sudden disappearance toward the south. As they slowly moved in that direction they took a zigzag path crossing back and forth to each little town and hamlet in the area. Sam was watching one man's reaction as they passed by a small village. He sat on his porch with a shotgun by his side, cussing the whole time while they passed; but he never made a move toward his gun, knowing it would be suicidal to attempt any such action. He seemed satisfied just to show his contempt for the Union army by his display.

The men had no trouble keeping warm during the day with all the marching; but when night came, it was a different story. Most of the time it was cloudy and cold with the occasional snow shower, but the worst night spent was one of freezing rain and sleet. Sam and his group tried keeping warm by a smoldering fire that struggled to burn in the wetness. Sam figured if he was going to be cold and wet, he might as well do it in his tent. The gum blanket he had draped over his shoulders was encrusted with a thick layer of ice and when he went to crawl into his tent he gave it a thrashing on the ground, throwing icy particles everywhere. He laid the wet side down for a bed and covered up with another. It was dry inside the tent, and he slowly warmed up as his body heat dried out the dampness. As he lay there in the dark, listening to the steady patter of ice hitting his little shelter, his thoughts went back to home and family; and how nice it would be to be keeping warm next to his wife.

With the coming of morning came the realization that no one was going to be moving today. Everything in sight was a glaze of ice, and you could not even stand up on a gradual slope without sliding away or falling. One good thing was the rain had stopped and breaks in the clouds meant some sunshine that may get rid of the ice. Another thing was that Sam had dried out nicely in the night, even his shoes. He kept them and his socks under the blanket near his stomach and that did the trick. His tent was like everyone else, weighted down to a slump with an ice and sleet cover. After getting ready, he crawled out of the flaps and cautiously got to his feet. There were men moving around camp but not very fast. The order for now was to hold this place until further notice. As the day wore on, rising temperatures slowly melted the ice away, enough to get traction for moving; and they were on the move again late in the day.

By the following night they were getting close to their objective. It was the mountains near Front Royal, Virginia. They would be turning back from this point after making contact with the enemy, if any were there. If there were Rebels, they would most likely be from the dreaded Jackson Corps. As they slowly approached near to Front Royal, the cavalry returned with news of the signal Corps being spotted in the mountains ahead, and that meant there was a sizable enemy command nearby, most likely Jackson himself.

Now they knew their columns had been spotted. It was time to start back to where they started. They waited until dark to retrace their steps, leaving the enemy not knowing where they went or why. They returned without any problems other than some nasty weather and sore feet, to take shelter back at winter quarters. With the reorganization of the army, General McClellan was gone and General Ambrose Burnside took his place. It seemed to bother many of the officers and men, but Sam didn't care much about that. He had just received a letter from Catherine. The baby was born on the 3rd of November. It was a girl, and she and her mother were doing just fine. That made Sam's day and in the evening many of the men shared their whiskey ration with him in celebration. Now it was the 10th of December. They were moving south. The roads were mud covered, and the march was hard and slow. By the time the XII Corp reached the Fredricksburg area, it was December 15th; and word came of the battle. The tragic loss of life was depressing to all, and Lee's army was in command of the field. Now it would be a winter standoff.

Sam spent his first Christmas ever away from home. It also happened to be his 29th birthday that December 25th, but it wasn't any fun. With the mud, bad weather, cold, and all the sickness in camp, it was depressing. January and a new year came. It was the 20th and the army was on the move or rather trying to move. Sam thought Burnside must have lost his mind, trying to move around Lee's army in this weather was mad. Every other man felt the same. It didn't work. For four days they moved, if you could call it that. The roads were gone. It was a sea of mud churned up by thousands. They came to a standstill on the 24th and went into hibernation. Winter camp was unspeakable—living in tents with the misery in camp and outside of it. They had to put up with harassment from the Rebels all winter. Sam was put on guard duty most of the time, rotating shifts. The worse threat was the enemy scouting parties and their snipers. That was scary.

With February came more snow and icy winds. Guard duty for hours on end was terrible in many ways. Besides just about freezing, you had to worry about getting shot from a sniper across the river. Some of the men were saying that they would get into conversations with the Rebs over the river, and it helped pass the time. Some were even exchanging things with them like coffee for tobacco. Sam never ran into that yet, until one early February evening as he had taken his post. He heard a voice call out from the other side. "Hey Yank! Stuck in the mud are you?" Sam ducked behind the nearest tree and kept quiet. Again, he heard the voice. It was in a thick Southern drawl he had never heard before that asked, "What's your name, Yank?" Sam hesitated a second, then said, "Sam, what's yours?" Then he heard a laugh coming from two men, and a reply saying, "That's my name."

The conversation did help him forget the cold somewhat and relieved the tension. The Reb called out to Sam that he was going to light a fire to keep warm, and said he hoped Sam wouldn't shoot in his direction. Sam said it was too darn cold to be fighting this time of year anyway. He watched from behind a tree, and sure enough he saw a fire lighting up the far bank and wasted no time in starting one himself. There remained an unofficial truce between the enemy lines the rest of the winter, and Sam ran into Sam many times across the river. One of their last talks had to do with the upcoming Spring campaign, and the last thing Sam heard from the Reb was, "Hey Yank! You better keep your head down once the fighting starts 'cause I'll be a looking for you." Time dragged on and on. This was known as Burnside's Mud March.

During the winter, Sam's mailing address was changed again. Now it was Second Brigade Second Division. The commander of the army had been changed, also. Now it was a man everyone called Fighting Joe Hooker. Sam liked the name.

With the coming of Spring, spirits were high. Things were drying out, and the April days were bright and pleasant. All the trees were budded and leafing out, and green views were pleasing to the eye. Again they were moving the army, heading southwest. The men were saying, if we keep this kind of movement up, we would be on Jeff Davis' doorstep before you know it. Sam was excited too, in less than a month he could go home. His nine-month enlistment would be up, and he walked with a spring in his step.

In the morning they came to a river and began to cross. When Sam was across, a sergeant was heard to say that the river was the Rappahannock. Sam didn't even try to spell it out; in his mind it was just another river. The long columns were headed due south and getting deeper into Virginia. Their new Corps commander was General Slocum. He was replacing Mansfield who died of wounds back at Antietam. Sam would not know either man if he fell over them. There was another river coming up, and they heard it was the Rapidan. They crossed and continued south. His shoes and socks were starting to get a little thin, now. He knew that much more walking would just about finish them off, and if he had to he would go home barefoot, just to get there.

All the men were worn out from marching as they came to a crossroads hamlet called Chancellorsville. It was April 30th and the XII Corps set camp at this place. The whole area in and around the crossroads was so thick with underbrush that they called it the Wilderness. Sam saw why it got that name. All the timber had been cut years back for lumber, and now a dog would have a bad time getting through that mess. The XII Corps was strung out from the main road to a high flat called Hazel Grove, just south of Chancellorsville, when on the morning of May 1st, some companies were moving to the road on reconnaissance.

They were not gone long when they ran into skirmish fire. It didn't last long, and the Confederates moved away. Sam was setting in his same spot as in the morning, when at 11:20 a.m. cannon fire began as he looked at his watch. The units that were out were ordered back and told to dig in for the night. The fighting went on all day. It appeared to Sam that it would be Antietam all over again, just in another state and time. Solid shot and shell were exploding continuously.

They stayed in their earth-works protected against most of the missiles. Men were being hit here and there by sniper fire, and the roar of muskets echoed in the distant woods all around, it seemed. Sam stayed put all day. There was no enemy close enough to shoot at but he could see at a distance gray columns moving through breaks in the trees. This went on until dark when the evidence of camps lit up the sky. At daylight the cannon duel started again. Their officers told them they could expect infantry any time that day and to be alert. They were in mass just to the south. Sounds of battle surrounded them again. The artillery fire kept them down behind their trenches and still no enemy to shoot at.

That night word was around that a major Confederate breakthrough happened just to the north, and things were uncertain. Sam could not believe it. He was being surrounded again, this time on a much bigger scale. The whole army was being swallowed up. How many men did Lee have? They seemed to be everywhere at once. That evening the Rebels moved in closer to the south of their position.

The morning of the 3rd was here and so were the cannon and Rebel infantry. They were told to start an orderly withdrawal, so they went with their rear guards out, every man looking back and firing as he went. They passed the Chancellor house that was starting to burn. The roads and woods were full of the moving men still fighting and running. They were trying to get to the river to set up new defensive lines. By the evening of the 4th, strong perimeters were formed and succeeded in holding back any Confederate threats. Some of the Union Army was already across the other side of the river, and the rest would be over by the next night.

More death and destruction and the army was demoralized again. Everyone was blaming the high command for all the trouble. Now things were at a standstill. As the army sat licking its wounds, Sam went through the quartermaster office to see about shoes. His sergeant said he would have them before he left. The next day the sergeant came back with dozens of pairs of shoes for men in need and orders for the 125th Regiment to pack and get ready to go home. With that a cheer went up that could be heard for miles.

They also found out now who had been shooting at them most of the time in their earthworks. It was part of

Jackson's Corps left behind to help cover his movement around the Union Army to the west. It pretty much succeeded by holding many troops in their positions long enough for the crushing flank attack to work. Sam realized the gray columns he had seen along with many others moving in the distance weren't a retreat as reported but the movement of Jackson's Corps for the attack that evening.

Now it was the 9th of May, and they were heading back to Washington to be mustered out on the 18th. For Sam and the rest, the fighting was over. He would be home by the 20th, for sure. They knew they had a lot of marching to do, days of it, and if they were lucky, they might be able to get a train from somewhere around Culpepper, Virginia, for the rest of the trip to Washington. The men laughingly said this march was one to look forward to. It would be their last and it would be taking them Home Sweet Home.

Samuel's first wife, Catherine, after the war, about 1872

CHAPTER 5

HOME AND BACK

On the morning of the 10th as they were finishing up their breakfast, they were hearing of the trouble that Sedgewick's divisions had gotten into, and the number of casualties the armies had inflicted on each other. The estimates were thought to be over 20,000 or more now.

They started to march in the direction of Washington. There were other regiments along with the 125th, whose time was expiring also. In camp each night the men and officers had to be on their toes. They were still in enemy country and would be under threat until reaching camp in Washington.

The losses were added up for the 125th Regiment, starting from their muster in to date. They had lost ninety officers and enlisted men, dead. This was resulting from battle action, sickness, and disease. The number maimed, crippled, captured, missing, and a few deserters were over twice that total.

It took several days to reach Washington, and they found the place very busy. They were assigned duty until their turn came on the 18th. There were just as many new troops starting out, as there were men finishing up. The afternoon of that day, they were on a train back to Harrisburg in route to Altoona. Once in Harrisburg, they separated for different destinations and said their farewells. The railhead here seemed just as busy as in Washington. Now they went west for Altoona.

Cheers and smiles went up as the train pulled closer to the station with all eyes looking into the crowd for familiar faces. The scene was full of hugs and kisses as Sam finally spotted Catherine and pushed his way to her with open arms. They hugged and kissed each other and stood for the longest time just holding their bodies close in a strong embrace. After a few minutes Sam stood back and started asking questions as he gathered his bags up, and they slowly walked away from the platform. He wanted to know everything that was going on with everyone and especially how she was doing. Before she could answer all his excited questions, she asked him how he was feeling, he looked so thin and care worn. Sam said he hadn't eaten very well the last few months and with all the action they had seen, all the men were lean and needed some home cooking to brighten up their situation.

He knew he wasn't his former self, but now he was home; and things were looking so much better to him. They talked as they walked towards their home, stopping more than once for a kiss or hug. Sam didn't like to talk about his experiences in the war; it was just something he wanted to forget. What he had told Catherine was things in general, and a lot of the gory details he kept to himself. He realized she knew it wasn't any picnic from what she had heard and read about the fighting. It was time to concentrate on other matters, letting the past be just that.

Within the week, Sam was back at the railroad shops again. They had his old job waiting for him, but there were many new faces now; partly because of the men who weren't coming back, and partly because of the demand for parts and equipment—the place was booming with business. Now at home, Sam had found out more about the statistics of his last battle and the death of one of the most feared generals in Lee 's army—Stonewall Jackson. He learned that he was shot by his own men the evening of May 2nd and died several days later. Ironic to go that way, Sam thought, but in that tangled confusion that existed there, he realized how it was possible.

The summer of 1863 was hot as just about all summers, especially in the shops at work with furnaces blasting, steam rolling, and machines all around. The temperature was unbearable, sometimes. But when Sam was home after work, he had time to cool down and enjoy his family. He kept up with war news day-by-day, reading about it in the newspapers. It was something that was upsetting to him, and he couldn't let it go.

The time went on with the daily routine of work and home when stories of the invasion of the North were heard all over. Lee's army was on the move again, and the safety of Pennsylvania might be in doubt. Sam kept up with all the current happenings day in and day out hoping something would be done and soon to stop this menacing threat. He knew the army now; he had been there and knew how things were done. That was what scared him the most. The problems with the leadership and the slow reaction time of decision-making and caution of the generals in charge of it all would probably be a total disaster for the North again. He knew how determined Lee and his army were and how fast they could move on any given opportunity. He had been there and seen for himself.

Now they were in Pennsylvania, in places as close as Greencastle and Chambersburg. The news was out, the state capital and other cities were targets for war, even Altoona could be hit because of the vital industry and railroad center here. News was they were headed east, concentrating between Chambersburg and Carlisle. The word came now about Gettysburg, Pennsylvania, and it was familiar news to Sam. He could picture it in his mind's eye what was going on better than most people. It may have been considered a victory for the North with the retreat of Lee's army on the 4th of July, but with that event the whole nation was in shock and in mourning. The call for more troops had been going on for a long time, and a draft system was already in effect. It had to be because the number of volunteers joining up had greatly decreased. The situation was on Sam's mind all the time. He wanted to get back in and help. It was a crazy thought, but he would go.

He was a veteran now and everyone knew it, but what outfit would he go with and when. The answer came to Sam soon enough. A man associated with the management of the Altoona Railroad shops had just been drafted and came to Sam to see if he would accept payment to substitute for his assigned service. Sam said he would think on it and let him know tomorrow. By this time Catherine knew there wasn't any stopping him. He was determined to get himself killed or be a hero, so she reluctantly gave her approval. The summer was ending, and Sam took another leave from work to prepare for war again. The man he would go in place of was from the Huntingdon County area. He had been assigned to the 149th Regiment, Company H, Pennsylvania Infantry. It was a special unit called the Bucktails. They were advanced scouts and sharpshooters, and that unit had already established quite a reputation for itself. They were now attached to the Second Brigade, Third Division I Corps, Army of the Potomac.

Once again Sam was on a train bound for Harrisburg. There he was registered with the 149th and supplied with more equipment. He had joined for three years this term and hoped he could return home on leave occasionally. Loaded on a train again, they were headed somewhere into Virginia to join up with the main elements of their Corps. The train was full of troops this time also, but the 149th didn't amount to that many men. He found out that they were replacements to bring the Regiment back up to strength, which were about 900 officers and men. All the men came from ten different counties throughout Pennsylvania, most of them mid to Northern ones. One man told him that when the battle of Gettysburg was over, one Huntingdon County Company had only eight men left. He thought maybe Company H, where he was assigned had all the losses.

They changed trains twice on their trip and ended up at Manassis Gap, Virginia, where they went into camp with the rest of their Corps. During the time Sam was out of the army, leadership changed hands again. Joe Hooker was out of high command and General George Meade was in, since before the Gettysburg battle. Now the papers were saying the President wasn't very pleased with old Meade's performance since then. Sam thought this army changed Generals more often than he did his socks. It was the 4th of October, and Sam was making friends fast, even though he shied away from it. Lots of the younger men looked up to him, because he was older and from a conversation a boy had with Sam, he found out Sam was not a newcomer to battle. All the new men in the 149th were looked upon as dirt or even cowards in the eyes of the hardened veterans, and they let that fact be known. The new men were harassed at every opportunity, and Sam knew it would stay that way until they could prove themselves worthy. He kept to himself and tried to ignore the insults. He liked this boy whose name was Jim, and that was all Sam wanted to know; but it was hard trying to avoid closeness when you were with these men all the time.

Now they were being called into company formation. Men dropped what they were doing, came running to the headquarters tents, and gathered in ranks before their officers. Jim was one of the last getting there, and he made a lasting impression on the head sergeant when he tripped and fell to the ground right in front of him. He jumped to his feet quickly, scooping up his muddy rifle, saw Sam and jumped into line beside him. The sergeant just looked at Jim and said, "Greenhorn, I won't forget your face."

At that he called out with a loud voice, "ATTENTION! The Company officers came front and center, and the Captain began speaking. He welcomed the new men to the outfit saying that they were now in the elite of the army, these Bucktails. He went on about their reputation and about what he expected from the newcomers. He was brief about it and returned to his tent with two lieutenants following in his wake. The sergeant dismissed the veterans, and as they left ranks they gave a look of disgust in the direction of the greenhorns. The sergeant stood in front of them. He was a large, burley man about 6' 2" with a natural look of meanness in his face. He had a deer tail pinned to the back of his hat like many of the other veterans wore.

Now he stepped quickly, stopping face to face with Sam, only inches away and stared into Sam's eyes. "What's wrong with your buddy?" he shouted, as he suddenly moved and knocked Jim to the ground. As he did this, he was cussing poor Jim the whole time. Sam could feel a sudden rage of pure hatred for this man filling him. He quickly got control of his anger and looked away from Jim sitting in the mud, all the time hearing the vets in the background laughing at them. Jim was not a very big man; Sam felt sorry for him and his embarrassment. The sergeant stepped back and said that some of them would be getting other rifles in the morning. "I will see you then. DISMISSED!"

They walked away, back towards their tents as Jim scampered alongside Sam, asking him, "Do you think he meant what he said to me?" repeating the question quickly several times. Sam said nothing and kept walking, still feeling sorry for Jim. He thought about the incident all evening, that it wasn't right to do such a thing to a scared boy like that. Let it drop; get some sleep, Sam thought to himself.

The next morning after breakfast, the new men were called into formation in front of the sergeant. A Corporal took roll call and told them to follow him; they were going to quartermasters to be issued new weapons. Sam and Jim turned in their old rifles. They were replaced with new ones that were different as they had a sighting scope mounted along the barrel. They collected them and went back. They went into formation, and the sergeant addressed them again saying, "I want you chicken shits to go with the corporal to get a feel for that rifle and report back here."

The Corporal called the men's attention to the new rifles they were holding. He made it clear that their permanent weapon would be just like that; but it would not have a telescope on it, and these were for special occasions. He said it was a Sharps rifle with adjustable sights, and the scope was graduated for distance adjustment. It was a single shot breach-loading weapon and was much faster firing than their old muzzleloaders were. The men all looked in amazement at them and inspected the new type of ammunition needed for it. They were shown how to operate the loading mechanism and how to adjust the sights for distance. The Corporal said any man who is not a good judge of distance would have to learn quickly, because his life would depend on it and many others to.

He went on to say that they were for long-range killing, and with the right man holding it, that it was possible up to a mile. After saying that, the corporal saw the men with wide-open eyes and mouths looking at him in disbelief. He continued by saying it was very good at close range battle because of the quick loading and the power it had.

The Bucktails were sharpshooters and did not like to be called snipers, as was so often used. Their duty to front line skirmishers would be held to a minimum, only if they were desperately needed. The Corporal said their job was to clear the way for the rest of the army by reporting on enemy positions and numbers while causing as much harm to the enemy as possible. They were to kill other sharpshooters, officers, cannoneers, and scouts of the enemy. Anyone who would help these operations was considered a target.

They were shown the special wooden cases that the scoped rifles were to be kept in when not in use and that they were carried in a marked company wagon. Their instructor said he would show them the turn in procedures when they finished practice, and they would get the regular sharps rifles back.

They went to an open field and took turns getting off a few shots at targets in the distance, while the corporal recorded hits using field glasses. When Sam's turn came he was a little nervous. The first shot kicked up dirt in front. The corporal just laughed, saying there was no need to look for that one. Sam calmed down, took his time and squeezed easy. "Direct hit!" said the corporal. The next two shots were within an inch of it. Sam knew they were good shots.

The corporal just wrote something down and asked his name. “Steel,” replied Sam and the corporal yelled, “Next!” Jim had already fired his shots and was waiting for Sam. “How was it? How was it?” Jim wanted to know. Sam didn’t reply. Jim said he didn’t do so well. Sam told him to give it some time. They were back in front of the sergeant again, and he was looking at the scoring report. “You damned fools all shot like old women, except for a few of you,” he said as he moved again towards Jim, who was at Sam’s side. Sam could hear him cussing in a low tone as he came at them. Sam felt the anger again, the hate for this man. He could sense Jim stepping back, knowing he would be the subject of abuse again. Then the sergeant’s eyes turned to Sam, and a split second later the sergeant and his papers were both spread out on the ground as quiet as a mouse. Everyone stood quiet looking in shock at what just happened. Officers ran to assist the sergeant, but he was out cold. Sam had hit him with a right hook that would have taken down an army mule. Sam was arrested and taken away for striking an officer.

About two hours later guards came to get him. He was being taken to Company Headquarters to receive his punishment. Sam was worried what might happen to him. When they got to Headquarters, he was sent into the tent where there was a long table with officers all around it and the sergeant standing there with a nasty looking eye that looked like the color of red grapes. Sam stood at attention, and a colonel at the table told him to relax; no one was going to shoot him. The colonel was from Division Headquarters. He had investigated the events that had occurred to see if a court marshal was needed here. He said,

"Sam! I have checked your past record and don't see a problem. Your record with the 125th is flawless." Right away everyone knew about the unit at Antietam. The colonel continued, "I think this matter can be overlooked this time, but Sam do try to take it easy on my officers, would you. We need more men like you in this army. Dismissed!" Sam left the tent and headed back, just a little puzzled.

As Sam approached his campsite, all the men's eyes were on him. Even the vets stepped back when he walked by. No one said a word to him, but there by the tent was Jim, jumping up and down all excited. "I thought I would never see you again, for sure! Thought they would throw away the key on you—I did, I did. Boy, Sam, that was something! Sure was. Everyone is talking about it. It's the talk of the whole camp now, Sam!" Sam didn't say anything. He just sat down to rest and look at that new rifle.

The next morning after they had eaten, there was roll call. The sergeant came in front of the men and said Lee was starting to move part of his army east. We may be expected to move at any time within the next day or so, so get used to the idea. It may be a hot one. I will let you know, as soon as I hear. With that he dismissed them except for Sam. He walked up to Sam and apologized for his acting that way, and said he had not known Sam was a vet. He stuck out a hand and the two shook. Sam started to say he was sorry about that giant bruise he gave him when the sergeant stopped him. "No time for that," he said, "I may be in need of you soon. Now go."

The morning of October 12, the 149th was ordered out in a hurry, going east. Word was Lee had moved around the Union Army and was heading for Washington. They had to head them off. It was a fast pace on a parallel route with Lee. They were ahead and were going to set up an ambush. Infantry and artillery were right behind them. Sam, with Jim along side, followed the lead of the Vets. They were put in a high spot overlooking the roads and fields but out of view, and the artillery backed by infantry was on the scene.

The morning of the 14th the Rebel Army was at hand. They had no idea the Union troops were there. Jeb Stuart's cavalry must not have been in the area, or they were just not seen; it was luck. When the time was just right, the order to fire was given, and the thunder roared with cannon and musket fire. They were caught off guard. The gray troops were dropping fast. Their officers were riding back and forth trying to organize a defense of some kind, but they were pinned down for now. Sam and Company H were in the best position to do the most damage, and they killed a number of Rebels, including officers. The fight didn't go on very long until the gray troops started pulling back to the trees and road; they had just come in from. The idea of visiting Washington would be put aside for now.

Supplies were brought up from the main element, so Meade's line was being extended. Company H was staying in place along with a battery and several more Companies of infantry. They were to stay there until the whereabouts of the Confederate Army, and their intent was known. That evening the men were ordered to stay in line and sleep on their arms. Guards were posted in front and in the flanks to give warning of the enemy approach, and things settled down for the night. Sam and Jim lay side by side in line covered only with the blankets they had and talked late into the night. As they lay there on their backs looking up at the sky, they could see every star in the heavens. It was a clear and chilly night, but they had no problem sleeping after the hectic day they had put in. At first light they were up shaking off the frost from the edges of their blankets, when a few more of their wagons were arriving. They were loaded with tents and camp equipment, and men were gathering to get things they needed.

Their officers said they would be here for at least a few days and to set up camp for now and report for duties. After a quick snack for breakfast, they were in formation being given instructions for details to be sent here and there. Company H was to proceed on a scouting mission heading east, then taking a turn south for one mile, and return back west to camp, taking one days' rations with them. The other companies were going in other directions. They headed out with the Vets in the lead and Sam and Jim in the back as rear guards. They passed through the countryside checking out every farmhouse, barn, and Hamlet as they went looking for any signs of the enemy. After about ten miles or so they turned south for a while. The sergeant went up to a farmhouse about this time and came back saying they would stay around here for the night, and the owner wouldn't mind. After checking the area out, they posted guards and rested. Sam and Jim were on duty first until about 2:00 a.m., when they would be replaced.

Things were quiet all night, and they traded off to take turns sleeping in the barn. When they were up and gone in the morning, they stopped about a mile out from the farm to eat and cook up coffee. Jim was grinning at Sam the whole time he was lighting the fire, and he had to ask what was so amusing. About that time Jim was taking these white objects very carefully from his haversack and smiling the whole time. They were eggs he had stolen from the farm. Now Sam was smiling, too. Fresh eggs for breakfast were quite a treat. They finished up and moved out again. By the time they got back to camp, it was nearly evening; and all reports were the same—no enemy spotted except the company that had followed in the direction of the retreating Confederates reporting old abandoned Rebel campsites about twelve miles out. They were to stay in place there with their Company and daily duties until further notice.

A few days later on October 19th, they were found. This time the Union cavalry, on scouting patrols in the Hay Market, Chestnut Hill, and Buckland Virginia areas, stumbled into a trap set by Jeb Stuart. The battle didn't last long. Most of it turned out to be a running fight. On a five-mile chase, the Union cavalry high-tailed it back to friendly lines. By the end they had lost 250 men. Most became prisoners. From that time on, it was known as the Buckland Races. Sam and the others thought it was quite amusing when they heard about it.

From October 20th until the first week of November, things were quiet. The men had plenty of time to themselves, writing letters, reading ones from home, playing cards and checkers, and trying to stay busy.

The last day of October was a cool, drizzly, and a foggy one; and it found Sam off duty, staying in camp trying to keep a fire going. He had just come off a four-day guard detail and wanted to take time to write home. Jim and his other camp buddies were on duty, and Sam had the place to himself for a while. He gathered more wood for the evening and stacked it by the fire, so it would be handy when it was time to cook; then he put more on the fire and went into his tent to read a letter from his wife. Catherine told him how much she was missing him, and it brought a tear to his eye and made his heart ache, longing to be at home. She told him about the children and how fast they were growing and learning how to get just what they wanted from her. This brought a smile to Sam's face and lightened his heart some. She went on to say that many people were asking about him and wanted to know about his situation. She told them what she knew from the letters and that seemed to satisfy them. She also said that her family was keeping a close eye on her, and things were just fine and ready for the winter there at home. This made Sam feel good, at least that worry about his loved ones didn't occupy his mind. Instead it was filled with other thoughts of war and just trying to make it through this period of his life.

After reading her letter twice and enjoying every word, he went out to stir the fire and warm up a little while he composed his letter to Catherine in his head. It was turning into late afternoon, and the drizzle of rain was about over. He thought if he was going to be writing, he better do it while he had good light to see and while he had peace and quiet before the others returned. So he crawled back into his little shelter with all his worldly possessions stacked at one end and stretched out to write. Once he got started, the words kept coming; and it wound up being quite a long letter, describing everything from battles to his friendships.

After finishing his letter, Sam just had time to take it to be mailed out before his buddies came back. It was just starting to get dark when they came in, and Sam had a good cooking fire going, much to their delight. As the men sat around getting dried out, they pulled their rations together and decided to make a sort of stew for the evening meal. Sam had already put some beans in water earlier that day, and they were puffed up and soaked just right. Jim had some salt pork and the others had a little dried beef and hard tack to add to it. After cooking it for a while, they added more water and salt, and then the hard tack biscuits last after they were crushed between two rocks. This made a kind of thickening or gravy to the stew and helped fill their stomachs. It turned out to be a fine stew for what they had to work with, and they all had a hot meal, which was a rare thing to have. Most of the time they were eating what little was on hand or what they could grab on duty or on the move.

They sat talking by the fire the remainder of the evening until fog and rain began moving in and sent them to their shelters for the night. As Sam lay in his tent looking out at the fire being slowly put out by the rain, he could see Jim's tent glowing from the light of a candle. He wasn't sure what he was doing and thought he must be writing to his folks to let them know how he was. While watching and listening to the rain patter on the tent roof, Sam felt sleep coming on, and he curled up under his blanket and drifted off.

Beginning in November, reports were that the Army of Northern Virginia had moved south, and Meade was going to follow it. On the 5th of November the cavalry and the 149th, for support, were ordered out headed for the Rappahanock River; and the rest of the army would follow along behind on the 6th. Their job was to push any resisters out of the way, and keep Meade up to date on things. For two days they moved heading south, running into an occasional enemy patrol. But the cavalry took care of the problem as they went along. When they got to the river, the main body was right behind. The cavalry reported on an enemy-occupied bridge ahead on the north side of the river. So with infantry, on a rare night attack, they took the enemy on while elements of the Union force crossed down stream at Kellys Ford. Lee lost over 2,000 men in the Union movement at the river and retreated to the other side of the Rapidan River. The 149th was involved in the night attack with some of its Companies, but Company H was on other duty. By the 8th, camps were set and once again things settled down.

The first week of November was gone now. The 149th settled into camp now between the two rivers as each day the weather grew colder. Jim looked at Sam and said it may be cold, but they had plenty of water. Sam didn't think much of the joke. The thing that bothered him was the bad winter that was coming on fast, and he dreaded it. He had experienced life in camp over the winter before in a tent and hated the thought of it. Even now, the day sometimes could be cold even with the sunshine, and the nights were uncomfortable after leaving the campfire. They got along as best they could with their daily duties and assignments at night. Some of their jobs, other than guard duty or a patrol, would be to help with watering and feeding the herds of horses and cattle, which was a break from the other boring things. Several times in mid and late November the rains came with sleet and snow mixed with it; and it really started looking like winter was here to stay. The food was always bad, and so many times the bacon they would get was rancid and green looking; the rice they had was full of large worms, and even the coffee had bugs of some sort in it. Things were not in the best shape for winter coming on. One day Sam and Jim had no duties, and camp was in good order. They had just spent that morning piling up firewood for a few days burning and had some clothes hanging to dry from all the wet weather from the previous few days, when they thought they would take a walk through the camps spread all around to talk to other men and see what was going on. It promised to be a nice warm day for a change, and they were going to take advantage of it.

As they strolled through each camp area, they heard and saw just about everything from poker games going on to boxing matches where they stopped for a while and watched a couple of big fellows going at it. There were crowds of men and even officers watching the fight, while wagers were being made on the outcome. When the blood started to appear on both fighters, Sam turned away. He had seen enough blood already in the army and walked away with Jim right behind. Jim caught up, and they went on a little farther when they heard the sudden blast of a number of muskets. They instinctively stopped in their tracks looking toward the sound, but there was no more shooting. Then they moved in that direction as other men were doing. When they got to an open field behind some tents, they saw it. Two men were on the ground twitching slightly with hoods over their heads. They had been shot to pieces by a firing squad in front of some officers and some other deserters that were watching. It was hard to look at, but these men had run away at least twice and were brought back. This time they were being made an example of to show the army meant business. They walked slowly away from the scene and returned to their campsite to enjoy the nice weather and what remained of the day.

November 26th came, and Meade made an advance to the north side of the Rapidan River where they met resistance from forward elements of Lee's army. The Union's I Corps was in the front line element with artillery and sharpshooters blasting away at Rebel forces holding the other bank. By the end of the day, the enemy seemed to be pulling back, and Meade wanted to cross in force the next morning. I Corps elements of cavalry scouts and infantry of the 149th led the crossing of the Rapidan. They were to push back any pockets of resistance, after crossing the pontoon bridge that was put in quickly by the engineering corps. The 149th followed the cavalry brigade across, followed by several companies of infantry.

Once on the other side, they spread out, advancing slowly as troopers on horses rode ahead just far enough to keep in contact with infantry and sharpshooters. Just about a quarter mile from the crossing, a few shots were heard just over a rise in front of Company H, and the rider came back in a hurry to report to Sam's lead officer. The rider then rode back towards the crossing. Now the officer turned and motioned to Sam to come forward. When he got there he was told to get two others and move forward to spot the enemy snipers. Sam grabbed Jim and one other man, and they went forward as the remaining troops took up positions. As the three of them crawled up the rise in front, they kept low as not to be seen. Sam looked at a tree line edging a small creek to the left and a field to the front with trees on the far end. As he looked he saw at least two men, one up in a tree at the creek and one more at the end of the field among the trees.

As he looked at Jim and the other man, they saw them too. Sam said, "I'll take the left; you two take center and right if we stir more up." Sam leveled off his rifle, took up a solid rest and sighted in his target. As he looked it over, he judged it 300 yards or more. As he watched the man in the tree, he knew he had no idea Sam was even there. Sam looked to his buddies and said, "On the count of: three: one, two, three." Smoke rolled through the grass in front of them as they watched their targets fall. The one in the tree hung for a second or two before falling twenty feet to the ground. About that time, they saw two more at the end of the field disappear back through the trees. Now the horseman was back and said, "Good job!" With that he moved ahead and they all advanced with him.

They had gone about a mile and were hearing shots in the distance, occasionally. Now they were increasing rapidly. The horseman returned, passing word to the lieutenant and headed back to the river again. This time their officer got them together with the other infantry officers and explained the situation.

With sharpshooters in advance, they would lead the infantry to first contact with Lee's advanced guard to test their strength. If it got too hot, they would retreat and wait for support or replacements. So they moved out along a tree line field. Sam was one in the front line as they went. He caught sight of movement to their front in a hollow in the woods. He yelled out to the officers, and they took charge of moving their men before the shooting started. Sam took cover behind a tree and began firing at every gray object he saw to his front while the rest advanced.

Now it was heavy firing from both sides. Sam and the other Bucktails kept up a brisk, covering fire as the officers ordered a fallback. Sam kept loading and firing with the other snipers as the infantry moved back to cover. The skirmish lasted about fifteen minutes and about ten men were killed or wounded. They had established Lee's location on the Union left and returned to report on their contact with the enemy and the results of it, but it was considered light and casualties were few. Within a short distance of the river, Lee's army was dug in and determined to hold their ground.

The 149th was sent back behind the line to the rear as a temporary rear guard unit and stayed in place there, while they listened to the thunder of massed artillery fire on the

Rebels and sounds from skirmishing going on here and there.

For five days, fighting raged back and forth with all the elements of war. But the stubborn Confederate resistance here at what was known as Mine Run was too determined. Now Meade pulled the Union Army back across the Rapidan on December 2nd and went into winter quarters.

CHAPTER 6

WINTER ON THE RAPIDAN RIVER

The weather was turning much colder now and with cold rains mixed with sleet and snow flurries making deep mud everywhere within sight. Forests were being cut down to supply the army with fuel for fires and shelters for the men. During December the army was reorganizing their Corps once again, and Sam was getting another new mailing address, so he would write to Catherine and let her know what it was now. It hadn't changed much. They were now in the First Brigade of the Third Division, I Corps Army of the Potomac.

Sam and Jim watched as men all around them were building log huts, lean-tos, and all kinds of shelter. They looked at their little tents and thought, no way would they live in them all winter long. They began to design their home for the many months ahead. They got with two other friends and shared in the work of building. With axes, shovels, and some rope, they could do it. Shelters of all kinds were being erected, and they used the best ideas from the combinations they had seen. They worked on it every chance they could, between duty hours while they stayed in their damp little tents. Tom and Bob were their building partners and would stay the winter with Sam and Jim. They got along together well and thought it a good team.

Tom and Bob were veteran soldiers as Sam was and had grown to admire him for some of his personal qualities. They came up with the plan and went to work on it. Tom and Rob, as they sometimes called him, went with axes to cut logs in the woods while Sam and Jim notched and stacked them. It took several days to get it up to the height they wanted, working on it in their free time. It was 10' x 10' square, kind of small, but it would be big enough to accommodate their simple needs. They had two openings in the square of the shack. One would be a small doorway, the other a fireplace hole.

They were anxious to get it finished, because the weather wasn't getting any better now in mid month. Now they could start their fireplace. They saw them all around, some made from wooden barrels, some from stones, and some from sticks and mud. They decided to make it partway with stones from the river, and the flue would consist of sticks and mud. Sam and Jim worked on the fireplace, stacking rocks and mud for mortar. Sam had Jim running about mixing the mud with field grass in it for strength as he laid the stones for the base.

Now Tom and Rob were back from duty and were starting on the roof framing, and by that evening the fireplace and roof were just about ready for completion. The next two days were nice ones to finish the mudding of the logs and fireplace and give it time to dry out good before they finished the roof. They all worked on building rough wooden bunk beds at the end of their shack, as they called it. Now they could finish their roof. They had to do it last, because they needed their tents stretched over the rafters to make a waterproof roof. With the remaining pieces of tent cloth, they covered the door opening and a small window opening at the one side they thought might be needed. Now it was finished—home sweet home, for the winter. It wasn't much, but it was better than a lot of the men in camp had to live in. The tent material on the roof let in plenty of light during the day, and one candle would allow you to see when it was dark. They moved in, bag and baggage, just in time before a heavy rain came, bringing with it sleet and much colder temperatures.

The next morning Sam was up early with the others. They all had early guard duty except Jim, so he made coffee for everyone while they got dressed for a miserable day with the weather. It was still sleeting outside, and it could be heard on the roof sprinkling down as they finished their coffee. Sam grabbed his gum blanket as he went out the doorway saying that it would help keep the wetness off some. Daylight was slow in coming because of the overcast sky and when the three of them made it to Headquarters tent, a lantern lit up the front. They were all gathered there tramping around in an inch of slush and mud waiting for their assignments. After being called into rank, Tom, Bob, and Sam were put on duty watching over horses and cattle and sent away to relieve the night shift. They were all in different spots about 200 feet apart making a perimeter in a very large field. When Sam got to his post, the man he was replacing was chilled to the bone, even though he had a small fire. He was soaked from the sleet and rain. He sure was glad to see his replacement coming and greeted Sam with a blue-lipped smile while trembling. He said he would help Sam get some wood for the fire; but Sam refused the offer, saying he could get his own and that the best thing now was for him to get back and take care of himself. After he went away, Sam thought to himself that if that boy didn't wind up on sick call, it would be a miracle. He gathered more brush and fallen limbs from the nearby woods and built the fire up some, standing in the slush, looking at the immense herd of animals, all intermingled, trying to graze on the sleet-covered grasses. As he watched them, he was amazed at the steam and vapor rising off their warm bodies, coming from their noses, and chewing mouths.

As the day went on, the temperature kept dropping and the sleet came down harder, slowly changing to snow with gusty winds. By the time Sam was being relieved of duty in the early afternoon, two inches of snow had fallen; and it didn't look like it would stop, any time soon. Sam was not one to complain, but his feet and hands were so cold, he was in pain. The walk back to camp got his blood circulating again; and when he got there, the steam was coming off his damp clothes like the animals he was guarding. When he entered their shack it was nice and warm. Jim had a good fire burning and a pot of stew cooking for them. It wasn't much, just beans and some freshly butchered beef. He had gotten them when he picked up their rations.

As Sam took off his wet clothing and soggy shoes, he listened to Jim talking as he watched over his pot. He said their company was being relieved of duty for several days and was being replaced by new recruits. That made Sam's day for him with this news, as he looked through his things for some dry clothing. He wanted to finish up before Tom and Bob made it back, so they wouldn't be in each other's way changing. When he finished he went to the pegs at the fireplace to hang up his wet gear, and he noticed something different hanging above it.

During the day Jim found time to make a little Christmas decoration. It was a wreath. Sam stood and looked at it in fascination; it was quite pretty. He turned to Jim and saw the smile of pride showing. He had gone to the woods for pine branches and cones and then tied them all together with grape vines and topped it all off with red bows fastened to it. Where Jim got the red cloth was a mystery, and Sam didn't ask. He knew Jim could find anything in this army, if he set his mind to it. Jim smiled again when Sam said it met with his 100% approval and was a delight to see. Now the other two were arriving just as cold and wet as Sam had been. They set about their business changing and warming up as they all talked about their day and what they might be doing on their time-off over the holiday in this kind of weather.

It was now Christmas Eve, 1863, and they had brought in enough firewood to last them a while, when Jim returned with letters and a package from home. Sam got a box of cookies and two new pair of socks with a nice letter. Catherine wished him a Happy Birthday and Merry Christmas and wished he were there. Tom and Rob both got letters that they sat and enjoyed. Jim had a sad look on his face; he had received nothing in the mail that day, so

Sam decided to pass around the cookies and read his letter again. It was so good to hear from home.

After finishing his letter twice, Sam looked at Jim munching away on those cookies, and he felt sad somehow for his little buddy. With that he reached into the box and handed Jim a pair of socks, saying, "Merry Christmas, fellow." Jim lit up like a ray of sunshine and smiled from ear to ear. They were warm and dry with a low fire burning in the fireplace that smoked into the room on occasion if it was windy. They went to sleep that night dreaming of home and family.

With the coming of the new year, January 1, 1864, there wasn't much to celebrate. The weather was terrible with snow, ice, and subzero winds. The only thing the armies both could do was to hunker down and try to keep warm. Other than an occasional pot shot at each other back and forth across the river, there wasn't a thing to do, except what camp entertainment they could find. January dragged on into February. In the first week of February, the weather broke into a little better temperature with some sunshine. Meade decided to wake things up a little by staging a demonstration on the Rapidan River. It went on from the 6th to the evening of the 7th. It was designed to throw a scare into Lee's army with the threat of an invasion. Cavalry forces were sent up and down the river with infantry marching back and forth and an endless artillery bombardment topping off the show. It didn't cause many casualties at all, but it did help stir the blood a little and relieve some of the boredom in camp.

The rest of February, March, and April were the same boring, dull routines with the only changes occurring when another new commander was put in charge, and Sam had received another new mailing address. It had now changed to Third Brigade, Fourth Division V Corps, Army of the Potomac. The army had reorganized once more. This time all the armies in the East, West and South were under one man with a new rank. He was Lieutenant General Ulysses S. Grant, whom even Sam heard of before. His reputation had started in the West and he was known to be a fighter.

April had started out chilly and it seemed to rain just about every day. Now it was the last week, and the sunny days were becoming warm and pleasant. Everything was drying out nicely, and wild flowers were popping up everywhere in the green grass. The trees were blossoming out and filling with leaves. The routines of guard duty and scouting patrols of winter were about to end. Word was they were moving in a few days, going south to find Bobby Lee's army. The new commander, General Grant had come down from Washington earlier to see for himself what the situation was with his other generals and let them know what he would do. He was going to travel with this army and not sit behind a desk somewhere.

On the morning of May 4th, the V Corps, under Major General Gouverneur K. Warren, was on the move crossing the river at Ely's and Germanna Fords on pontoon bridges with the 149th spread out ahead as an advanced guard. Sam and the rest of Company H were close enough to the bridge at that time to see the thousands of men, horses, wagons, and artillery cross over. They would be replaced soon with other men as the following Corps came up. The Bucktails waited, and then were ordered to the advance of the V Corps. They were moving into country now that Sam remembered from the year before. It was the wilderness—a place that brought back some bad memories. This time he was coming in on the north side being followed by over 120,000 other troops. The 149th was divided up into three company groups and ordered into the woods and thickets between the Orange Plank Road and Turnpike to report on enemy positions and strengths.

It was well into the day by now; and Sam, with half of Company H and their 1st Lieutenant, went to the left of the Corps along side the Plank Road. The only thing they had to report that evening was the sighting of Rebel scouting parties that disappeared into the woods in front of them, with no contact being made. The lieutenant left for headquarters and had the men stay where they were for the night, and he would be back. Through that evening they could hear the noise of gathering troops to their front in both directions. They lay there quietly listening when about 9:30 the rest of Company H returned with more infantry from V Corps and settled in on the right from Sam.

A few minutes passed and a sergeant Sam knew so well now, appeared with some other familiar faces and came up to him quietly. The sergeant asked Sam to report what was happening, and Sam filled him in. "Sergeant," Sam said, "I don't know who they are, but there sure seems to be a lot of activity going on in front of us. I could hear sounds of infantry moving around and talking in both directions, right and left, and we heard a shot being fired about ten minutes ago. I don't know if they spotted our line or not. I don't think so; no return shots fired. I think one of them Rebs tripped his trigger by accident and shot into the ground while moving in the dark. By the sounds of the movements, it is just infantry; I heard no horses or wagons at all, but there sure seems to be a lot of them moving out there. I think they are settled in now, and occasionally I just hear muffled voices. I would guess there is at least two Regiments directly in front and possibly two more right and left."

The sergeant listened to Sam's every word, then looked around in the dark, saying nothing for a minute. Then he spoke in a low tone, looking at Sam, saying "If you make it through the Spring campaign and keep up the good work, I want to put you in for a promotion." As they talked, Jim was standing in the background grinning. The sergeant told the group they were facing Ewell's men out in front and to expect the worst in the coming day. With that he went off. They sat in the dark that night ordered not to have fires, just eat their rations.

Jim sat by Sam as they ate and talked quietly in an excited voice. "Sam, if you don't get your darn head shot off in the next few weeks, I may be taking orders from you. What do you think of that?" Sam looked at Jim's smiling face and just groaned, then said, "Let's get some rest; I have a feeling we are going to be busy in the coming day."

When daybreak came they were all on alert, anticipating shots to be fired at any moment, but it remained calm. The rest of the morning passed without incident, but the presence of the enemy could not be overlooked with the sounds of activity coming to them from all directions. It was just a matter of time before the tension of waiting would be over. At about 12:15 p.m. the sound of muskets started on their right. It was slow starting, but grew in volume and intensity within minutes. As the sounds moved in their direction, the order was given to move out.

They moved slowly through the tangle. Now they could see them up ahead and knelt to fire a volley on command from their sergeant. "FIRE!" was the last word heard as flame and smoke poured from the line, now the opposing line and back and forth with the brush being cut by lead all around and men dropping with every blast. As they fired rank-by-rank and reloaded, the order to advance was given, front line first in order. Sam and Jim were close in the second line as they advance with bullets filling the air. Now it was becoming confusing in the thicket with all the smoke and noise. Orders were being shouted that could not be heard clearly, and it was every man for himself now. The organized lines a few minutes ago were now everywhere, staggered all through the woods, men advancing into the smoke and men coming back out. Sam could see the heat waves rising off the barrel of his rifle as he took a minute to look around in the direction he would be shooting next. As he reloaded he saw men in gray moving in every direction as well as blue, and he saw Jim to his right firing and knocking a Rebel down in the smoke to his front. More Union infantry moved in behind their position, and the firing in front from the Confederate lines was increasing.

They were running low on cartridges, and the order to fall back was passed down the line.

After that Sam found himself behind fresh troops in line ready to move up. It went back and forth a long time like that without gaining any ground in any direction, and bodies were piling up in the leaves. After catching his breath with the rest of his line and receiving more ammunition, things were beginning to slow down somewhat. The musket fire had settled to a few steady scattered shots. Now during the lull in the action more troops were moving in, and supplies of ammunition passed forward to the men holding the woods in front. Now Sam's 1st. lieutenant was there and wanted him and about a dozen men to go with him around to the left for reconnaissance to see what was up. They moved to the left through the thicket for a long way, not running into any enemy until they could see an opening of sunlight and fields. At that point, about half the group stepped out into the sunny opening to look around with field glasses and scopes for enemy elements in the vicinity. Sam grabbed the lieutenant's arm and spun him around saying, "Look at that, Sir!" They were about 200 yards away from a small clump of trees at a roadside and saw a cluster of men staring back at them. They knew right away they weren't combat troops, but who? In an instant, the lieutenant knew they were officers and staff all alone in this field.

Now they were moving around in a hurry; one on a horse stood out. He had a distinguished look with a large plumed feather in his brimmed hat; and he moved quickly from his partner under the shade tree, who was dressed in a clean gray uniform, wide-brimmed gray hat, and shiny black boots going up past the knee. As he mounted his gray horse they watched his gloved hands grab for the reins as horsemen gathered round to shield him. As they quickly moved away, they could see the white hair and beard glisten in the sun.

The lieutenant ordered them back into the woods, and they stood looking at one another in amazement that no one even raised a rifle to the enemy. It was something unexpected and strange. They now realized they had stumbled onto a meeting of officers in the field, and two were identified without a doubt as Jeb Stuart and Robert E. Lee.

It was a missed opportunity that everyone was just now starting to realize. If only they had fired a volley in the direction of that group of officers, most or all of them would have been wounded or killed before escaping. Just the thought of the possibility of killing or capturing Robert E. Lee and some of his top commanding officers would have been incredible. They all began talking, speculating about the outcome of their lost opportunity if they had only reacted faster to the situation. Their lieutenant summed it up without using any wasted words. He simply said that it would have ended this battle for sure and possibly the war with such a loss to the South. With that said he ordered flankers to move out, and they would start their movement back to their lines.

After moving through the thick woods about 200 yards or so, movement was spotted on their left; and it wasn't men in blue but an enemy scouting patrol. As far as they could tell they hadn't been detected yet, so the lieutenant ordered a skirmish line formed just in case they came that way. They formed on a slight rise of ground in the woods that might afford some cover, then waited and watched. From Sam's position on the line, he could see flashes of light-colored figures moving through breaks in the thicket and knew almost at once that it was coming right at them. Every man in line knew it now, but there was only a dozen of them in this spot and no friendly troops in sight.

The Lieutenant spoke quietly, saying, "Steady boys, fire on my command." A chilly tingling sensation went up Sam's back, and every nerve and muscle in his body was ready for what ever happened. The worst thought on everyone's mind was what he were facing—small patrol or half a rebel army. No one knew. Now it stopped; all movement and images seemed to disappear like a ghost. Had they gone in another direction or were they in a place just out of sight? The short time the silence lasted seemed like forever. The only thing heard was one's own breathing and heart pounding.

There they were again, seeming to appear out of nowhere, right in their sights. With the loud shout of the order to Fire! it could be seen that the enemy flinched in reaction to the surprising suddenness of it—and now came the blast. After reloading and the smoke clearing away, there was no enemy in sight. Only three that weren't so lucky remained motionless in the leaves. It turned out that it was a Rebel scouting patrol about the same size as their group, and they had quickly retraced their steps back to where they came from. Now the Lieutenant said, "Let's move out before they return in force and give us more than we can handle.

They returned to their lines once again, and the sound of a larger battle came back to their ears. It was increasing again in the same manner as it had earlier that day. The Lieutenant stopped short of their earlier position and placed them in the skirmish line to the extreme left of the army in contact with the other fighting units. Sam and the rest were separated from their Regiment, but that wasn't the problem now. It was the enemy moving in front of them and threatening to take them over. The Lieutenant parted the group, leaving them with their hands full.

It seemed like forever, shooting and ducking bullets until the rest of their Regiment finally joined them in the action. Low on cartridges again, Sam went to the rear when he was relieved and took a much needed break. With his head thumping with every beat of his heart, he lay on his back trying to count how many Rebels he had knocked down. He didn't know for sure if they were dead or not, but this time he counted six for sure.

CHAPTER 7

ADVANCE TO LAURAL HILL

Now there was a new element to deal with other than the musket fire from the Rebels. Fire was breaking out all through the woods everywhere. The smoke of gunpowder was thick enough; but now clouds of wood smoke was filling the air, making it difficult to breath and see what was going on. The hot sparks from the muskets firing had set the dried leaves on fire, and the underbrush soon went up like a torch.

As Sam lay on the ground trying to get some air, he could hear screams from the wounded men in front of him, as they were being burned alive by the spreading flames. Many men were down from both sides with injuries and loss of blood so bad, they could not escape the flames. The fire was coming very close to Company H's position in the woods. Now the men in line were looking for some kind of order from the officers on what to do next when the order to advance was given. Sam gazed at the others with a look of wonder on their faces and then back at the flames just to his front. The heat was getting pretty intense, and in a few minutes flames would be on top of them, so he got to his feet, spotted a hole in the fire and dashed through, holding his breath as he went.

After he had gone about thirty feet or so, he was free from the worst of it, but now was in a world of smoldering, blackened earth with small torches of flame hanging all around from tree tops to ground level. As he moved ahead slowly, he saw men to his left and right advancing with him. A volley shattered the haze to their front, sending a sheet of lead at them; and they hit the ground instantly with moans coming from their lines. Sam could feel the missiles whizzing past his face before he went down onto the smoldering body of a man whose clothing had burned away, leaving the blackened figure in the ashes. Now the Union line let loose with a hail of lead, and it was soon answered from the Rebel line. This time dirt flew in Sam's face from the rounds hitting the ground in front of him. He knew he could not stand up and run forward, so he dragged two bodies together rolling one on the other in front of him for cover while he reloaded on his back. There were many more exchanges of fire over the next fifteen minutes or so; and with every volley from the enemy, Sam could hear the thud of the bullets hitting his protective wall of flesh.

Every opportunity he got, he would point and fire into the thick clouds of smoke to his front. Only on occasion was it possible to see a target or some kind of movement to shoot at in hopes of doing some damage. The firing was becoming a constant, unbroken roar to the ear and with the rush of loading and firing; it was difficult trying to concentrate on the job at hand. His mind did not pick out any distinct individual sounds at all; it was just a mingled, jumble of sounds, not being processed by the brain.

Their line was running low on cartridges, and the three rounds Sam had left were a deciding factor in what to do next. He looked to his front, picked out an image and fired, not taking time to see the results, while rolling onto his back and loading one of the three remaining cartridges. At this point Sam was undecided on just what to do. Should he conserve his ammunition in case of a Rebel charge on their line? If this happened, it could mean the difference between living or dying or becoming a prisoner of war. As he lay there on his back thinking of what to do, the answer came to him quickly. An officer from somewhere behind him shouted, "Here they come!" Sam rolled back in a position to shoot and saw the gray line moving right at them. Again the situation was desperate. The firing from the Union line seemed to melt away the charging foe, and Sam was down to one last shot when the advancing lines turned and began a withdrawal. At the sight of this, Sam sank back down and let his heart slide back down his throat to its normal place in his chest.

Things were starting to quiet down some, when a new line of blue came surging forward and past Sam's line. It sure was a welcome sight to the tired, blackened survivors. They crouched low and headed to the rear. All of them were getting low on ammunition, and many had burns and singed clothing from the heat of the passing fires. Now they were far enough away to set down, rest, and take in some much needed water. It was hard to believe, but many men fell asleep even with the noise of fighting all around them.

Now the sun was getting closer to the hills in the West, and the firing was slowing with evening coming on. Just as it started getting dark, three companies of the 149th, what was left of them anyway, were moved to the edge of a field on the left flank as night perimeter guard and ordered to sleep on their arms with every 3rd man taking turns staying awake until dawn. As Sam was taking the first shift, he looked around and watched as the sky glowed with an orange light from the many fires still burning out of control. When he was relieved from his watch, he walked in the dark to the edge of the field, and lay down and was asleep in no time.

The men were all ordered up at 4:30 a.m. that morning by the last man on guard duty and told to eat, because they would be moving soon. Sam stretched out in the nest of grass he had slept in and dug into his haversack that was getting empty and found some hardtack and old cooked bacon pieces and ate. As he sat up and looked around, still chewing his meal, his eyes were starting to get adjusted to the darkness. He could make out black images behind him. It was other men straining to get underway for the day. He was sucking on a bite of hardtack trying to soften it a bit when he noticed some odd looking, light-shaded objects next to him in a line on the ground. As he sat and ate, he kept looking at them and becoming more curious as the objects became clearer. He got up and walked over to the first one for a better look and saw a skull sticking from the leaves, then another, and then more. He became wide-awake once he knew what he was looking at, and then the earth gave way underfoot. He had stepped down through the ribs of a dead man. As he removed his foot, he saw the bony feet wiggle in the leaves. As he walked away, he could not think of anything but those poor shoeless, bony feet and the terrible battle that had raged here the previous year. They were buried in mass graves in a hurry and not very deep. The seasonal rains had brought them to the surface. Sam wasn't the only one to discover that many of them had slept in and around a burial site.

At 5:00 a.m. elements of three Union Corps were moving to their left, right in the same area where Sam and the group had seen Lee the previous afternoon. Now they were fighting on their right and front again and advancing on Hill's Corps on the Orange Plank Road. They were engaged immediately, smashing headlong into the enemy lines. Fighting broke out in every direction. After about two hours of intense battle, they had gained some ground pushing the Rebel Army back with massive charges, killing and capturing many enemies and losing many themselves. About 11:00 a.m. sounds of fighting were on three sides of Sam's company. They were getting hit from Longstreet's Corps on the left flank, and the roar of battle was deafening. Straining to see through the smoke and pick out targets was very hard. The only thing to do was point at gray movements and fire. There was no stopping to rest. It went on relentlessly for hours. Sam could hardly see with sweat running in his eyes, bringing with it burnt, black powder residue that was all over his face and neck.

Now the order came to fix bayonets and charge. As Sam came to his feet, a feeling that someone had tapped him on the shoulder with a small tack hammer went through him, but he never stopped in his movements and ran forward with the rest of the men. At around 2:00 p.m. things began to quiet down some, and during this lull in the action they were ordered to dig in. The officers were determined to hold this position or else!

Now he heard Jim's voice saying, "I've been looking for you old buddy. How you doing?" Sam looked around and replied, "I don't exactly know. I've been pretty busy." As they worked together piling up rocks and wood, trying to make cover, Jim said, "What's this?" looking at his right shoulder. Sam looked and his jacket was torn there, and he noticed a burning sensation. He removed his jacket and shirt and saw he had been grazed by a bullet right on top of the shoulder bone, just enough to bust the skin and bleed a little. Jim said with emphasis, "Boy, are you lucky! A little more to the left and you wouldn't be so tired now." They finished their work and rested, emptying their canteens of drinking water and washing out their eyes.

Now it started again. A smashing counter attack that saw men fall by the thousands once again. It was mostly all infantry fighting, because artillery units could not see far enough in the woods to be effective. So it was back and forth the rest of that day, into the darkness, before the killing would stop. After the fighting stopped, the 149th, along with other regiments, were replaced on the front lines and sent to the rear where they rested from two days of hard work.

The morning of the 7th saw part of the V Corps moving out, along with elements of the other Corps. They were moving to the left and away from Lee's army. A lot of the men thought it was a retreat, and they had been whipped again; but when they turned south and kept going, they thought different. They were headed to a place between Lee and Richmond to cut him off at Spotsylvania. As they moved away that morning, they could still hear the sporadic sounds of battle in the distance.

At the breaks in the march, Sam, Jim, Tom, and Rob all found each other and were glad of it. They were together that evening of the 7th of May when numbers of casualty estimates were being told about camp—11,000 Confederates and about 12,000 or more Union. It was sad to hear such a thing as that, but still the spirits of the men seemed high. They were missing quite a few men themselves, and they didn't know whether they were on other duty or dead.

As they sat and talked, they all agreed to do some cleaning up; and a small stream close by would serve nicely. Their bodies and uniforms were encrusted with road dirt, soot, and ash from the fires and gunpowder residue. Their jackets and pants were soaked from sweating, and white salt residue was streaking dried lines all over with the smell of body odors and sulfuric acid. It was quite unpleasant. They removed their shoes and waded into the chilly water, socks and all, and laid down soaking their sore feet and bodies.

It didn't take long to get used to the chilly water, and they washed the best they could without soap. They soon had their clothing off and thrashed them about, rinsing and squeezing out clouds of dirt. They then hung them on bushes to start drying and went back into the refreshing water. Jim told Sam it felt so good, he wanted to stay in all night. But there were others waiting, so they finished up and returned to the campfire to dry everything more thoroughly. As they dressed piece by piece that evening, they talked as they ate. It sure felt good to get cleaned up after two weeks of being so uncomfortable.

The men started talking again as they sat around the fire. They couldn't help but notice that Tom was awfully quiet as he looked into the fire. Sam asked, "Tom, is there something wrong? You aren't saying much." He looked up from the fire and answered, "This will be my last night; I have that feeling about it. We have been through a lot of tough scrapes lately and are lucky to be alive, but this time I have my doubts about me making it." Sam said, "We all think that at times, but you will be fine. Don't worry so much." With that thought in mind, they decided to write home while they had time. Jim put more wood on the fire, so they could see a little better to write. As he watched Tom put his name and address on a slip of paper and place it in his pocket, he heard Tom say, "This way they will know who I am when they find me."

They had all heard of men doing this type of thing, for a good reason. So many bodies had been recovered that were no longer recognizable, even to their best friends, that it seemed a good idea to do so. After a little thought on the matter, they all did the same.

As Sam was writing his letter home, he could not help but notice the change in his feelings towards this war and all the dying that was going on around him. It was starting to become routine. He was not bothered by death like he once was, and the thought of being use to it was scary in itself. He knew his wife had to know the change in him also, without saying it in so many words. It was hard to be cheerful in writing a letter home under these conditions, but he tried his best and told Catherine all about what had happened and where he was. Like all the men, he loved receiving a letter, because any news from home had to be better than what they faced every day.

They were all waiting for the mail to catch up to them; they had been on the move so much lately that finding the different units was a slow process. When they finished their letter writing, Jim took them to where they would go out with the rest of the mail in a day or so. When Jim returned, Sam had coffee ready and they all sat and talked again of family and home. This seemed to help Tom's mood somewhat, and then it was time to rest. They went to sleep on the ground with their rifles at their sides, and Sam went to sleep with his shoulder stinging a bit.

The next morning after breakfast and roll call, stories were going around about some of the past fighting. One of them was of several men being killed and when their rifles were picked up at the spot where they lay, their ramrods were still in the barrels. That wasn't too unusual, but the strange thing they discovered was the barrels had from four to six rounds stuffed in them and had never been fired.

Now came word that the hills in front of Spotsylvania were occupied with artillery and infantry. Somehow Lee had beaten them there with night marching on a more direct route. Neither of the main elements of either army was there yet but would be coming within the next day. Now they moved closer, then stopped to hear back from headquarters what the next step should be. While they waited, Sam and the others could see across a wide-open field that sloped gently up hill from their position in the woods. It must have been a thousand yards to the farthest tree line where most of the gray activity could be seen. The other trees to the right ran away at an angle and nothing could be determined for sure.

The Rebels had picked a very good position for defense; and as they stood there looking in that direction, they thought to themselves—that's a long way to go in the open. About 11 a.m. on the 8th, word came back from Warren's command that the artillery on hand would have to support the infantry advance, and that Laural Hill must be taken before it got any stronger.

While the men waited, they tried keeping their thoughts off what had to be done by talking, eating, pacing, and even sleeping. Sam had a bad feeling about the outcome of this advance on the enemy lines and tried to brush it aside by thinking of things at home. He was wondering how things were growing in the spring garden and if the new green shoots were up through the soil yet. He was wondering how much help his wife was getting from family and friends and how the children were doing. He was deep in thought almost to the daydreaming stage when he was brought back to his senses by Jim tugging on his jacket sleeve and saying, "We are going to form up in a few minutes out in the field there; I thought you would like to know."

Laural Hill, Virginia, near Spotsylvania. This is the field where Samuel was wounded

At noon the artillery opened on the Rebel positions on top of the rise. There were only four of them and firing long range just now, but more guns were on the way when the 149th and two other regiments were ordered forward. They came out of the shadows of the trees and started across the fields with their own artillery rounds whistling and hissing over their heads. As they moved forward they could hear the exploding shells up ahead. Now they could hear the pop and crack of sniper fire. At that, the sergeant of Sam's company said to spread the ranks and run straight for a depression in the field. Once they got there they were to lie down to assess the situation. No cannon fire had come from the gray line yet, just sniper fire taking out a few men. From this place, the Union snipers were of no use. They had to go up to the right, to the tree line that ran at an angle, to get a place to fire from.

While the Union cannon kept the Rebel gunners ducking, the 149th moved to the right of the depression while the rest of the infantry held fast. From the right, Company H and D now were sent to get a position in the woods at the top. From there they could have a chance at the artillery personnel. With support from two other companies of men, they might take that position and make it much easier for the rest to come on. They lay there ready to go just as the cannon fire was at its peak. They stood and ran through the field, just about 200 men rushing an unknown tree line. Jim, Tom, and Rob were all sprinting alongside Sam, running like they never had in all their lives, when musket fire broke the trees in front at about 100 yards. They knew now it would be a troublesome thing getting there. They all stopped in line and fired into the woods as a volley came right back at them, knocking men down.

With a reload they were running again; as they got closer, more detail came into focus in the trees. Sam saw he was charging straight at a cannon only about fifty yards away. Just as he was going to yell at Jim to change to the right, the canister blast came. Grape shot caught Sam in mid stride and as his left leg went to touch earth; he fell still in stride, coming down on the shattered bones of his leg spearing them deep into the earth and falling forward. Though still listening to the shots being fired, he was dazed and wasn't sure where he was. When reality set in, it was with an enormous amount of pain. He rolled over and propped himself upon his elbows and watched as the last of the Union soldiers went into the woods.

They had taken this weakly defended position for the time and ran off all its defenders, except for the dead and a few prisoners. Now Sam looked down at his leg again. It felt like a thousand bees were stinging him below the knee, and a deep, dull ache was moving up into his hip. Some of his own men were moving up to him with prisoners in tow. He could see others in the field checking survivors. Now the sergeant was kneeling beside him and waving over some help. He was reassuring Sam as they were carrying him away, that it would be all right. There was a man under each of his arms, clasping tightly to his wrists as they went around their shoulders, and he hung limp between them. Now things were becoming fuzzy and blurred. He could hear them talk as they went. The last thing he heard was, "Not much leg left," and something about blood loss.

When he opened his eyes again, the first thing to come to his attention was the pain in his left leg. He lay there on his back trying to focus his vision and tried to get up, but the weakness in him was so overwhelming that it was difficult to raise his head or arms at all. He was totally disoriented, not knowing where he was or why he was like this. As his mind began to work past the terrible pain, he began hearing sounds all around, moaning, and screaming seemed to fill the air. Again he tried to get up and only succeeded in raising his head far enough to see the source of his pain. Through his blurred eyes, he could see blood soaked rags wrapped on his lower leg and men moving all around in a hurried pace. He lay back again and turned his head from left to right seeing the same thing in both directions—men everywhere attended to by stretcher-bearers, aides, and surgeons. As he closed his eyes again, it all seemed to be a dream. None of this made any sense to him at all. Where was he?

Now a voice came to him saying, "How are you doing, Private?" As he opened his eyes he saw a man looking down at him from a distance, and he repeated the question. Sam tried to speak, but nothing seemed to work. His tongue and throat were so dry he could not form words to answer the man. He knelt down to Sam saying, "Here, drink this. It will loosen you up and help with the pain." The water was warm, but it took the burning out of his throat; and he drank as much as he could, and then gasped for a breath. As he continued drinking, with his head being propped up, the man put a bottle to his mouth in place of the canteen as he said, "This will help the pain some." It was a chalky, bitter-tasting liquid that soon was washed away by more water from the canteen. Now the man stood up, with grass and dirt particles falling from his pants, as Sam realized he was lying on the ground. As the man was starting to leave, he placed the canteen at Sam's side and said, "You drink as much as possible; you have lost a lot of blood and are dehydrated. If it weren't for the tourniquet the aides put on your leg, we would not be talking now. Get some rest, and I will be back to see you later. Sam was starting to get drowsy, and the pain was letting up just a little as he drifted off to sleep.

He was awake again, this time he was bouncing up and down being carried on a stretcher to another location; still in so much pain it took all his strength to withstand it. He was taken to a larger tent this time, filled with other wounded soldiers; and then was told his leg was amputated. By this time his thinking was much clearer, and he was remembering all the lost details of past events.

For several days he remained in the same place, receiving food, water, and occasional attention from aides cleaning him up and giving him medicines for healing and pain. Then after about a week, he was loaded in a wagon with other wounded and sent off over the bumpy roads towards a Union hospital near Fredericksburg, Virginia.

The trip to the hospital was agonizing to all the passengers. With every bump in the road, moans would be heard coming from the ambulance wagons in the procession. When they finally arrived, several men had passed away during the trip and were taken away for burial.

After several more days of lying in pain, a surgeon came to see Sam and told him about the gangrene that had set in on the tissues in his stump, and that he would have to operate again and cut away all the diseased tissue before trying to send him back north for more treatment and care.

After this second operation, Sam started to get back a little more strength; but the pain was constant with him, and after about a week he found himself back in another bouncing wagon heading north to a train station that would finally deliver him to Washington and another hospital for treatment. In Washington things were just a little better, but the crowded, smelly conditions were only relieved by something Sam had not seen before. They were nurses and volunteer women who showed more compassion for misery than he had received before.

After an extended time there with better food and care, Sam could feel his strength coming back slowly, and again he would be moved to yet another hospital. This time he was loaded on a train destined for Chester Hospital near Philadelphia, Pennsylvania. As the train rolled along heading to the Northeast, Sam was thankful to be getting back into Pennsylvania and was happy with the help from nurses in getting a letter off to his wife about his situation. It had been a long time since she had heard from him, and he knew it had to worry her deeply. He didn't know whether the war department or one of his officers notified his family of his being shot. He wanted to write to her himself and inform her what was going on with him, instead of her receiving just a cold form letter from the army.

Once again he was put into the care of a Union army hospital and informed by a surgeon he needed more cutting on his stump. This was the last thing Sam wanted to hear. He was just starting to be able to deal with the remaining pain, and now he had to endure another operation. The thought of it made him sick to his stomach.

The surgeon had already examined him, and now took the time to explain what needed to be done. He unwrapped the bandage from Sam's leg and pointed out that the bone was extended too far past the muscle tissue, and that there wasn't enough skin left to stretch over and close up the open wound that was left by field hospital work. Sam didn't have much choice in the matter. If he wanted to live, he would have to go through whatever it took to keep from being eaten up by the gangrene. The very next morning Sam was taken to where the operation would take place, and the surgeon reassured him he could get enough skin closed over to allow for proper healing.

Again the thought passed in Sam's mind as it had many times before: How would he live with the loss of that leg? Would his wife still love him? How would he be able to make a living? What would it be like having a wooden leg and crutches to move about on? Could he make it; would he survive this test?

Now he was being put to sleep, and everything in the room seemed to melt away. He could feel coolness, first on his forehead and then it moved down to his cheek. It brought his eyes wide open with the suddenness of it. He focused his eyes, looked around, still not quite in touch with all his senses, and found a smiling face looking at him with a hand holding a cool glass of lemonade. It was Martha. He was back now on his front porch. Martha didn't say a word, and neither did Sam. She went back into the house, knowing he had just experienced that vivid dream again, one he had several times a year ever since the war. It would probably continue until his dying day.

Samuel G. Steel, between 1885 and 1890

ABOUT THE AUTHOR

Gary Steel was born in Altoona, Blair County, Pennsylvania. In 1951, the author moved with his family at the age of one to a farm in Huntingdon County, Pennsylvania. At age 8, the family moved again to Everett, Bedford County, Pennsylvania where he finished his schooling, graduating from Everett High. He is the youngest of six children to wonderful parents. He became interested in the building trades at an early age and spent over 30 years working at them. Along with other hobbies, he has always been fascinated with the Civil War and his ancestor's part in it. The information obtained for this book prompted him to have a memorial brick placed in the Walk of Valor, located at the National Civil War Museum, Reservoir Park, Harrisburg, Pennsylvania.

www.ingramcontent.com/pod-product-compliance
Ingram Content Group UK Ltd.
Pitfield, Milton Keynes, MK11 3LW, UK
UKHW040015200726
13854UKWH00001B/223

9 780759 695214